The Relationship Dance

A Guide to Loving

Gracefully

GWiz Publishing

Published in England
by GWiz Publishing
(A division of The GWiz Learning Partnership)
Oakhurst, Mardens Hill, Crowborough, E. Sussex. TN6 1XL. UK.
Tel (+44) 1892 309205

info@gwiztraining.com

www.gwiztraining.com

First published 2018.
10 9 8 7 6 5 4 3 2 1

ISBN: 978-0-9955979-0-7

Contents

Acknowledgements

We would like to thank the following people for their help and support along the way:

- Graham Browne: For the inspiration behind the dynamic of advancing and retreating energies. He helped us to understand and break old, unhelpful patterns. He also shared ideas with us on how to redefine our boundaries in relationships and how to stand up straight!

- Friends and colleagues that we have spoken to about how they 'do' relationships. You are all exemplars… and so you have now become part of our modelling journey!

- Folks who have attended our courses and workshops and have asked amazing questions and challenged us to refine our models. Also, for their stories, comments and observations.

Foreword

The BIG question

There is a question we are often asked, sometimes out of curiosity and sometimes out of exasperation: *"How do you work together?"*

It is as if some folk can't get to grips with the idea of a married couple happily working together too! And first things first, we *do* work together but we have our own separate businesses too. But for us to sit at the front of a room and run a course together without arguing or falling out seems to be a marvel and a miracle to some. The key answer, we believe, is that we enjoy it! It makes us laugh. If we didn't enjoy it, we wouldn't do it.

Even when we told people we were writing a book about relationships together; the most common question was: "How?" The answer is simple (though the details took a while): contracting, complimentary (and complementary) collaboration and balanced-constructive communication.

Key Pointer: In our relationships, let us hold *equal* authority, take *joint* responsibility and make a difference *together* as we engage with the world outside in all its wonder and its challenges. *We are on the same side!*

Another telling question was: "Who has the final word... Melody or Joe?" Now, this can be taken quite literally (i.e. who writes the final word in the book) but the question was really about decision making, authority, power and control. These can be important factors in a relationship. Whether consciously or unconsciously, most of what people do in relationships is about feeling in control (or to *avoid* feeling 'not in control'). In terms of who has the

power/control in our relationship, wherever possible the answer is...
'us'!

About the Book

Within this book, you will find ideas, models, strategies and
activities. The important thing to remember is that this comes from
the authors' joint 'map of the world'. Nothing we say in this book is
absolute truth; it is based on our uniquely filtered observations.

This book is a culmination of the models, tools and strategies that we
have developed as a result of living life and experiencing
relationships (both our own and through the observation of others).

In the development of our own models, we have also drawn
inspiration (and adapted ideas) from diverse areas of psychology,
transactional analysis, gestalt, neuro-linguistic programming and
Virginia Satir's family dynamics. Where possible (and where ideas
are not our own) we have endeavoured to source other people's
material in a 'further reading' section in the back.

Whilst the book is in nine chapters, it could also be considered three
sections:

1) Chapters 1-3. Sets the scene and establishes a plot.
2) Chapters 4-6: Lays the foundations and builds the structure.
3) Chapters 7-9: Creates the space for the relationship dance.

Terminology

As you read The Relationship Dance, you will find certain
terminology that we have used in our models and throughout. For
example:

- **Balanced**: when we talk about a 'balanced' relationship, we use this as an overarching term to mean equal, healthy, happy, successful and harmonious. As the opposite to balanced, we use the term 'unbalanced' to mean 'not balanced', 'out of balance' or 'potentially unstable' where someone is perhaps adding more to (or taking more from) the relationship than their partner.

- **Energy**: When we refer to energy, we are talking about a dynamic of advancing or retreating. The term energy is used as an analogy (we are not talking about energy in an esoteric sense), to give a feel of movement (i.e. pushing towards or against vs pulling away or back). We are endeavouring to 'quantify' how much someone might be advancing or retreating, i.e. how much energy or effort they might put into it and to what extremes.

- **Constructive**: instead of using the word 'positive' or 'negative' we use the terms constructive or destructive. We are talking about the building (construction) of a relationship and its maintenance over time. We talk about behaviours that help to build and behaviours that tend to threaten the integrity and ultimately bring down relationships.

- **Pathology**: when we talk about a person's pathology, we mean their psychological weaknesses or compulsions.

- **Ecology**[1]: Whenever a person makes a change in their behaviour, thinking patterns or emotional responses, there is likely to be a ripple effect. The changes will impact on those we are nearest to. We recommend that when making changes, you consider the 'ripple effect' and take steps to manage the impact on those you care about. In so doing, you can avoid unwanted and unintended consequences.

- **Positive intention**[2]: Everything we do is driven by an underlying desire to have something or to make something

The big picture answer to strong and healthy relationships is rather simple. Indeed, beyond just love, perhaps *all you need* is a combination of the following:

- *A degree of self-awareness*: understanding your own processes and reactions to situations. Being able to *stop* yourself and sometimes give yourself a good (and kind) talking to.
- *An awareness of others*: understanding how other people feel and how they are likely to react... an ability to empathise. This also includes being able to predict that when we behave in particular ways, there will be a certain reaction or response (emotional/behavioural) from our partner.
- *A desire to make the relationship work*: being motivated enough to change some of your ways... to do what it takes to make things work for you *and* your partner... so that you *both* get what you want. It is not just about what *you* want to get from the relationship but also, what are you prepared to give? We don't necessarily mean that you have to compromise, but rather to create an environment that provides greater fulfilment for you both.
- *A range of communication strategies*: finding the most effective approaches for ongoing, active communication with your partner, from keeping them up to date with what you are thinking and doing, through to expressing what is truly important to you in the relationship... and of course being 100% prepared to listen to what is important to them.

The Relationship Dance

A couple of years ago, we decided to learn how to dance. We took lessons in Ballroom and Latin style and soon found that whilst it was challenging to co-ordinate our steps, there was a lot of fun and laughter! We even perfected our own unique steps which we called the 'Captain Jack Waltz' (talk to us if you want more details!)

It became apparent as we 'took the starting hold' that the dance was an interesting metaphor for a model we had been developing, about how couples advance and retreat within their relationship. It gave us ideas about creating a balance point where a purposeful partnership could move 'to and fro' in harmony and synchrony.

It has always fascinated us that when we run training courses together, we often hear the same comments from our audiences. People are keen to know if we argue or compete with each other; they wonder if we score points off one another!

We found this very puzzling as it didn't fit our shared map. We work collaboratively, building on ideas together. We also genuinely admire one another and enjoy observing the other succeed.

This difference between our map and the expectations of many others triggered a curiosity within us. We wondered what patterns were running in our relationship and what patterns were being 'projected' our way by others.

This led us to researching various models of relationship in different schools of psychology. Particularly influential was the work of John Gottman and his *Four Horseman of the Apocalypse*[3]. This model describes many of the behaviours our audiences were expecting to see when a couple worked together (i.e. dysfunctional!) Building on our research we began to see a set of alternative patterns that could be useful for people wanting to improve their relationships and/or change unhealthy patterns.

The Relationship Dance is a bringing together of the simplest steps and routines we could find to make the biggest differences in people's lives and their relationships.

The Relationship Graces

To dance with grace is have balance, poise, form and dignity.
To communicate with grace is to have tact, etiquette and manners.
To love with grace is to have compassion, generosity, good will, kindness,
tenderness and responsiveness.

How can couples create a space and environment in which their relationship will thrive? In our study of how effective partners behave towards one another, we began to see that it is not just *what* the partners do but *how* they go about it. It seems as if they act from some (usually) unspoken 'ground-rules' which give them a platform to 'dance', to communicate and to love with grace.

From observing and discussing the 'ground-rules' with successful couples, we developed a set of *high-level agreements* which we called the **Relationship Graces**. These agreements will help you to create a strong dynamic where you and your partner can address issues and needs without fear of ridicule or rejection. These agreements will affect **how** you communicate for the life-time of your relationship. They will determine potentially how you approach challenges and differences, how you treat each other and how you behave towards each other. These agreements will enable you to discuss ideas, challenges, plans, decisions and actions in the most constructive way.

And what happens when the 'ground-rules' are not in place? The answer is a list of classic relationship problems... incompatibility, irreconcilable differences, conflict, contempt, familiarity, boredom, blame, argument, disrespect, selfishness (at the expense of loved ones), drifting apart, too much pressure from outside (e.g. work) and within (e.g. neediness), lack of 'quality' time for one another and lack of shared interests and goals. The couple may experience a deep sense of uncertainty and insecurity.

The five Relationship Graces (Care, Kindness, Respect, Compassion and Dignity), as outlined below, are our version of the 'ground-rules'.

When we commit to these agreements, we live and communicate *together*, remembering always that *we are on the same side, even when we see things differently.*

1. **Care** *(ongoing maintenance)*
   We will place purposeful attention and effort into caring for and developing our relationship. We will continue to make the maintenance of our relationship a high priority, no matter what else happens in life.

2. **Kindness** *(open communication)*
   We will speak our truth with kindness and listen to one another even when the topic is less than easy. We will always be willing to communicate with one another.

3. **Respect** *(constructive action)*
   We will act constructively towards one another, particularly when it comes to our differences. We will speak respectfully about one another when we are with others.

4. **Compassion** *(balanced expectations)*
   We will act to meet each other's needs as well as our own and we will endeavour to be balanced in our expectations of one another.

5. **Dignity** *(joint ownership)*
   Without blame, we will take ownership of our own feelings, thoughts and actions. We will hold ourselves to account in staying with these agreements.

Chapter 1

The Dynamic Relationship

Will you, won't you, will you, won't you, will you join the dance?
Lewis Carroll (*Alice in Wonderland*)

In This Chapter...

In this chapter, we will be introducing the idea of 'advancing' and 'retreating' in relationships. You will have an opportunity to reflect on whether *you* are sometimes an advancing or retreating energy. We will then go a little deeper to determine how we develop our patterns, templates and models in the first place, that we then use for our adult relationships. We will also begin to introduce the 'solution' to the 'problem' of an out-of-balance dynamic.

We will be exploring the following questions:

- What is the difference between a 'balanced' and an 'unbalanced' relationship?
- How do you know whether you are an advancing or retreating energy in your relationships?
- Where do we learn to dance and how do we choose a partner?
- Why do unbalanced relationships last?
- How do we dance with love, balance and grace?

Introducing the Dance

In many ways, a love relationship is like a dance. When the relationship is healthy, we stand in the middle of the dance-floor and with permission we step forwards and backwards in harmony with one another, often returning to the middle. As a couple we flow, in balance, sometimes leading and sometimes following.

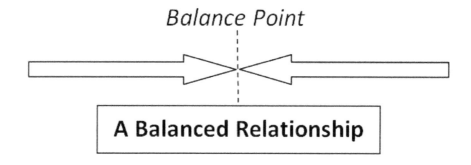

However, when a relationship is less than healthy, there becomes an imbalance. Sometimes only one person leads, either pushing or pulling a partner who doesn't necessarily want to go where they are being led. Alternatively, as one partner advances, the other retreats, so the first advances more and the second retreats more. They end up off the dance floor, perhaps with the retreating dancer pinned up against the wall. But to some, even this may seem better than sitting alone by the side of the dance floor

We (the authors) call this 'dance' the **Advancing/Retreating Dynamic**. When a person is a perpetually *advancing energy*, they may do so because they need connection; they want to be with their partner, to see them, to talk with them and to sit right up close to them. On the other hand, when a

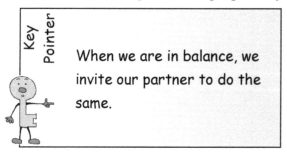

Key Pointer

When we are in balance, we invite our partner to do the same.

person is a constantly *retreating energy*, they usually need their own space, to have time alone; they want to be able to breathe.

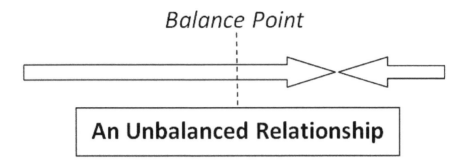

It could be argued that both energies in the dynamic are about gaining and maintaining *control*. The advancing energy may attempt to take over and own the space and the retreating energy may simply 'allow' them to do so. The advancing energy may want to reach across and get a reaction from their partner. Their retreating partner might just back off further.

A Case In Point

Whilst this is not about a love relationship, at the start of my career I remember having to travel to work with a talkative colleague. She would insist on driving, listening to her music and talking at me for an hour and a half each morning. What did I do to control the situation? I said I wasn't really a morning person (or an afternoon person for the journey home) and I would remain quiet and reflective. She would tell me that I was being very quiet, was I okay? I think to her I appeared sullen and remote. Since being silent didn't really work so well, I ended up falling asleep! Who knew that falling asleep could be a control mechanism!

Joe

Some couples flip back and forth between these energies and so a harmony is maintained. However, the issue arises when the two become permanently out of balance. The retreating energy finds the advancing energy smothering, threatening and perhaps suffocating; they want to step back and escape. The advancing energy feels abandoned and unloved; they want to step forward and fill the gap.

In real terms, the advancing can happen physically (wanting to hold hands, touch and hug), mentally (talking at and sharing their views, opinions, thoughts and ideas) and emotionally (expressing joy, upset, anger etc.). Retreating can also be physical, mental and emotional. Indeed, it is possible for someone to be, for example, a retreating *emotional* energy but simultaneously an advancing *mental* energy. The advancing/retreating dynamic tends to be context specific; for example, we might have one partner who advances where finances are concerned and the other advances when it comes to designing and decorating the living space. Indeed, we might apply the **Advancing/Retreating dynamic** to many areas of the relationship, for example: money, parenting, housework, DIY, cooking, sex, interests, television programme preferences...

How do you know if you are Advancing or Retreating?

Whilst you may already know where you advance and retreat in your relationships, have a look at the examples below and decide where you would be (i.e. to what degree might you be advancing, retreating or balanced).

Advancing		Retreating
Texting 20 times a day.	....	Phone switched off.
Following partner from room to room.	....	Closing doors.
Asking for reassurance (e.g. "do you love me?")	....	Unresponsive to love talk.
Constant talking.	....	Silent treatment.

Creating lists/ instructions for partner.	....	Following instructions (or ignoring instructions).
'Nagging'.	....	'Forgetting'.
Interrupting as partner talks	....	Unresponsive as partner talks

It is possible that we may consider ourselves advancing or retreating but encounter someone who is the same but more extreme than us; we might get 'out advanced' or 'out retreated'. This can throw us into the opposite energy.

As an aside, a *highly* extreme example of advancing–retreating might be domestic violence, where one partner is physically/verbally abusive and the other disappears for days without contact.

Where do we learn to dance and how do we choose a partner?

It is likely that we learn the relationship dance at a very early age, from our parents and other significant caregivers. If the template we see and learn is healthy, we will probably have a better chance of finding and creating balanced relationships later on.

It all comes back to *patterns* and *modelling*. As children we observe the world about us in order to make sense of it. We tend to look to our mother (or female care giver) to show us what a woman is like and our father (or male care giver) to understand men.

If our parents are our main role models early in life, we are likely to model our same-sex parent and hence form a partner-template based on our opposite-sex parent. Now before you get squeamish and accuse us of being overly Freudian, remember we are generalising here. Of course, children grow up in different family dynamics, but the point is, our family will dramatically affect our templates for the future. Some people find attractiveness in the same-sex template and others either form a counter-template or do not work from the parent template at all.

Consider your relationships past and present. Think about the physical characteristics of people you find attractive (e.g. height, hair colour and eye colour) or their 'personality' (e.g. warm, cool, friendly, aloof etc.) Notice any connections?

You might now be thinking: "Ah! But my partner is the exact opposite of my opposite sex parent!" However, that is also kind of the point. Sometimes we rebel and go for someone who is the complete opposite of our parent! We are still being motivated by the *same* model.

A Case In Point

When doing my first degree in psychology (and philosophy), a fellow student was taking the opportunity to question the scientific validity of psychology as a field. Whilst I agreed with some of his points (indeed, I think of psychology as a 'fuzzy science'... a matter of probabilities rather than absolute laws), I changed the topic and asked him about his girlfriend. I then asked him to tell me about his previous girlfriend. He admitted he was attracted to a certain type of girl. You may be ahead of me here... I asked him to describe his mother. He didn't get very far before appearing somewhat confused because he was using exactly the same descriptors, both physical and emotional. I can't remember discussing psychology with him again after that!

Joe

As an aside, this selection process seems to hold true whether we are 'straight' or 'gay'. It is just the basis of our pattern; sometimes a gay person may develop their template from the opposite sex parent and build an attraction model on same the sex parent... or vice versa!

It is not uncommon for relationship patterns to be mirrored from generation to generation. For example, there is much written about the likelihood of a child of an alcoholic growing up to either become an alcoholic or, perhaps more puzzling, marry an alcoholic.

A great example of this is detailed in the writing of the author Robin Norwood[4]. She was the daughter of an alcoholic and married two alcoholics in a row herself. In her books she shares her recognition of patterns that drove her choices unconsciously. Her second husband was not showing indications of addiction when she met him and yet at the unconscious level she recognised and chose someone who fitted her pattern. Her awakening to her patterns resulted in a journey of self-discovery that allowed her to break her patterns.

The likelihood is we will be attracted (unconsciously) to someone with the compatible energy to us. For example, if we are balanced, it is likely we will find a balanced energy. If there is an imbalance we would tend to seek an opposite energy (e.g. advancing chooses a retreating energy and retreating chooses an advancing energy).

Why do relationships with unbalanced patterns last?

Unbalanced relationships can last because on some level it works for both of the people involved. It is as if two people bring their pathology to the relationship and create a joint pathology! It doesn't mean they are happy, just that their expectations are fulfilled. We take the view that a relationship is only a problem if the people involved consider it a problem. You need to evaluate your own relationship and if it works for you and your partner then it works regardless of the opinions of others (including ours!)

Of course, many couples stay together for life as extreme advancing and retreating energies. They fulfil each other's pathologies and so they 'fit'. However, although this may 'feel right' on some level, it may be less than rewarding on others. Consider the couples that stay unhappily married simply because they 'fit' one another.

Does this mean two advancing energies couldn't relate to each other? They can, although they may find themselves in competition with one another and bumping against each other. And two retreating energies might live quite single lives whilst being married.

Consider this: people who grow up with a balanced model of relationship are more likely to experience a balanced relationship themselves in adulthood. However, some long-term relationships might be considered unhealthy but still last the distance due to the mutually interlocking patterns. In other words, *longevity in a relationship is not necessarily an indication of a balanced relationship.*

A Case In Point

For the first thirty years of my life I was extremely unhappy in relationships. I had some very jaded beliefs about love; I suspected that love didn't really exist! I thought it had been invented to sell books and films!

I looked around and all I could see were people who seemed to have unsatisfying relationships where they did nothing but complain about their partners. Those people who "claimed" to be happy, I didn't believe!

I seemed to attract men who were consistent in one thing, their lack of respect for me and their ability to be emotionally and psychologically abusive. In my early twenties I got married to a man who I do believe loved me in his way but was still abusive emotionally and at the end of the relationship was also physically aggressive.

Around the age of twenty-nine I got to a point where I said to myself "there must be more to life than this!" This is the point where I embarked on my own journey of personal development. I started to realise that I was making choices about partners that led to my experience. I was only drawn to people who would treat me as I expected to be treated and I "filtered" out men who did not fit my expectations.

I was moving away from being a victim to my life and toward taking ownership. As I became more aware of the level of choice available to me my sense of self became stronger.

My choices had been driven by my early experiences and the patterns created at the unconscious level. By making the unconscious conscious I could examine and change my automatic processes leading to healthier outcomes.

I discovered that by learning to love and like myself my expectations changed. I was no longer attracted to abusive men. I started to notice "good" men who had always been there, some I had even rejected because in my old map they were labelled as "weak".

I thought they were weak because my original model of a man was that he should be aggressive, dominant, demanding, controlling and unlikely to share his feelings. The men I had overlooked were sensitive, respectful, assertive, had healthy self-esteem and shared their feelings because they wanted to.

I often hear women saying things like "there are no good men out there!" This is not true, what is more likely is that the women making this statement have blinkers on preventing them from noticing the great men right under their noses!

The great news is that by changing my map I was able to open myself up to a healthier balanced relationship. One in which I behaved in a healthy way and the man I chose did the same. It was at that point that I met Joe. We have now been married for twenty-four years. We are also business partners working together every day.

Melody

How do we dance with love, balance and grace?

The first step is to return to the balance point. In this section, we are giving you an overview, i.e. the model. (Later in the book we will be exploring the 'how' of stepping back or forward.)

If you are an advancing energy, step back to the balance point and give your partner space.

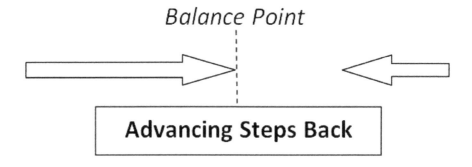

If you are a withdrawing energy, step forward to the balance point and engage with your partner.

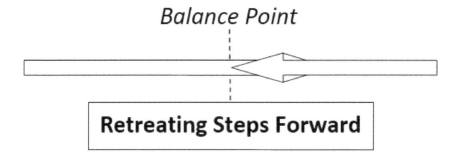

The interesting thing is that it only takes one person to change the dynamic. If you return to the centre of the floor, your partner will need to return back in order to continue dancing.

Of course, this is sometimes easier said than done. To go against our template and conditioning may feel less than comfortable, or perhaps even a little scary. For some, it may feel like too much of a risk. What if I step back to give my partner space... but then they *don't* step forward, fill the space and return to the balance point? Or, what if I step forward and embrace my partner, only to find they embrace me back and won't let go?

A Case In Point

When we first began living together, I often woke up in the night to find that Melody was right over my side of the bed. I was moving further and further to the edge, and Melody would (in her sleep!) move closer to me. I would end up holding on to the edge of the mattress getting more and more frustrated and unable to sleep. (The comedian Lee Evans did a piece about the same thing where his wife was taking up the whole bed and he was hanging on... to the pavement outside!)

Now of course I had options, including getting out of bed and going around the other side where there was plenty of space. However, instead, I turned around and held her. She sighed in her sleep and then returned to her side of the bed! If you are an advancing energy, you might be thinking: "And?" but as a retreating sleeper, it took a strange amount of will and effort (battling my own frustration and facing an illogical fear of being smothered). Remember that this was not about Melody; this was about my own pathology... What if she had grabbed me and never let go? But she didn't... and I knew this on a 'rational' level... however, pathology can run deep.

Joe

The thing to remember is: if the advancing energy steps back, it may take a while for the retreating to trust and step forward. Likewise, if the retreating steps forward, the advancing may take a while to step back. This can be challenging for both parties.

Health warning: it is important to consider the ecology (consequences) of a *sudden* step forward or back. The partner who wants balance may need to do some 'pacing and leading', taking it one small step at a time rather than dashing back to the centre of the floor. Where appropriate, the partner who wants balance might choose to communicate how they feel and what they want: "This is where I'm at in our relationship and I'd like us to..."

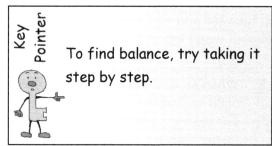

Key Pointer

To find balance, try taking it step by step.

What if our partner isn't prepared to change step?

Now we have the tough bit. If one partner desires change but the other partner absolutely doesn't, then the first person has options (for example: return to how it was before or change partner). If the relationship is working in every other way, is the 'partner-desiring-change' prepared to live with things as they are? Unless someone is in a highly destructive (e.g. aggressive/abusive) relationship, we might encourage them to try out a range of different moves (e.g. communicating differently) before leaving the dance altogether. However, if the other partner is simply *not* prepared to change and all other options have been exhausted, it may be time to move on.

There is an important dance lesson here though: before finding another partner, it is beneficial to learn to balance one's self. For those who are normally the advancing energy, they will need to find ways of being self-sufficient and happy in their own company. For those who are normally the retreating energy, they will need to be open to intimacy (and prepared to share their space). Without *personal* balance, a person may well find themselves with a new partner who has the same old dance moves as all their previous partners.

Where else does this apply?

The advancing/retreating dynamic has applications beyond love relationships. You can just as easily play out the dance in the workplace. A 'micro manager' who wants to know the details of everything you are doing can feel like an advancing energy. The manager who is hard to get hold of may feel like they are retreating.

As well as your love relationship, consider some of the other relationships you have. What is the dynamic you play out with children, family, friends, and with people at work? When, where and how might you benefit by returning to a balance point?

Enjoy the dance, for without the dance, there is nothing.

Chapter 2

Balance, Attachment and Interdependence

(A Deeper Understanding)

"Sing and dance together and be joyous,
but let each one of you be alone,
Even as the strings of a lute are alone
though they quiver with the same music...
And stand together, yet not too near together:
For the pillars of the temple stand apart,
And the oak tree and the cypress grow not in each other's shadow. "
Kahlil Gibran *"The Prophet"*

In This Chapter...

In this chapter, we will be making connections between Bowlby's attachment theory and the balanced relationship. We will then move on to the nature of dependency and interdependency.

We will be exploring the following questions:

- What is an attachment style?
- What is the difference between balanced and unbalanced attachment styles?
- What is the relationship between dependency and unmet needs?
- How might we develop interdependence?

Whether we are in a relationship or not, we need to know how to 'balance' ourselves. In order to do this, it can be helpful to gain a deeper understanding in how we got to where we are now and then how to get to where we would like to be.

Attachment Style in Adult Relationships

During the 1960's, psychologist John Bowlby[5] was interested in child development and in particular how children developed an attachment style with their parents. The style developed was related to the type of parenting the child received. In a nutshell, he identified three labels for attachment: Secure, Ambivalent and Avoidant.

Bowlby's labels equate neatly to the 'advance/retreat' model discussed in the previous chapter:

1) **Secure equates to Balanced.**
   Securely attached adults are more likely to have good self-esteem and trusting long term relationships. They will share feelings with friends and partners easily and comfortably. They will also feel comfortable in seeking out social support. They are most likely to be attracted to someone else who is also securely attached. These are the relationships that are most likely to be happy. A secure child is more likely to naturally experience secure attachment in relationships.

   When we feel secure, we know where we are with one another. We feel safe and this allows us to do more and to explore (together and on our own). The Five Relationship Graces (see Introduction) are designed to help couples feel a stronger sense of security (and certainty) in their relationship together. They will back each other up and will look out for one another.

2) **Ambivalent equates to Advancing.**
   This style could be described as "needy" and the individual may spend a lot of time worrying that their partner may not love them. They can become extremely distraught with the notion of a relationship breaking up (to the degree that it could be described as obsessive). Paradoxically they may also be reluctant to become close to others. So even though they fear their partner does not love them they may passively reject their partner. Descriptions of "clingy" and over-dependent are also given to this attachment style.

3) **Avoidant equates to Retreating.**
   The avoidant style may have problems with intimacy and be reluctant or unable to share feelings and thoughts with others. They may invest little or no emotional coin in social and romantic relationships. They will avoid intimacy by making up excuses such as tiredness and may not be concerned when a relationship breaks up. They may appear to move on straight away. They may also be unsupportive of a partner who is experiencing stressful times.

One observation we have made is that ambivalent types often find avoidant types attractive and vice versa! This seems to provide a guarantee of dissatisfaction in the relationship but also familiarity!

Why revisit Bowlby? Our intention in re-visiting Bowlby is to start looking at patterns and see where these are leading us in our understanding of adult love relationships. We suggest that this as a journey of hope. For those of us who were not fortunate enough to grow up in an environment that fostered secure attachment *there is light at the end of the tunnel*.

Unbalanced attachments: Interlocking patterns and dynamics

An interlocking pattern is usually an unconscious dynamic where a couple are locked or 'hooked' into a way of being together. It is usually compulsive and unhealthy. However, interlocking patterns can create a long-term relationship.

Whilst we have been focusing primarily on an advancing/retreating dynamic, there are other interlocking patterns that can appear to work for some couples:

1) **The Competitive Dynamic**: In this dynamic, both partners are up to the mid-line and continually pushing the other. They will compete for air space, for living space, for awards, to win, to out-do and to be better than. At worst, they will put each other down and ridicule each other. At best, they will cheer each other on and admire one another whilst still striving to be better than their partner!

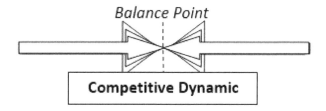

2) **The Remote Dynamic**: In this dynamic, both partners retreat to their own space. Perhaps they don't spend much time together, or don't talk much or touch much. They may both be content with this.

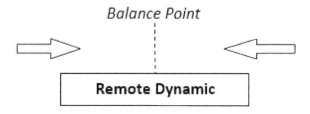

A Case In Point

A couple I worked with were in this 'remote' dynamic: he was in the Navy (posted away) and she lived at home alone. This worked rather well for them and the times they were together were exciting and 'urgent'. She would drop all other activities while he was on leave, and they experienced the 'honeymoon phase' all over again. They were intense and spent all of their time together.

However, when he retired after 30 years of marriage and service, things changed. The pattern of living meant they were now together every day. Sustaining the intense 'honeymoon' pattern was exhausting. The wife began to feel smothered and controlled, even though her husband was not really being invasive. He also felt enormous pressure to pay attention to her. They eventually reached crisis point and finally admitted to each other how they felt. They realised that neither of them was happy with their new pattern. They needed to make some changes.

After some heart and soul searching, they found that they did indeed love one another, but it took some serious negotiating and communication to get to that point.

Melody

3) **The Co-dependent Dynamic**: In this dynamic, the couple seem close and supportive to one another. However, when you look closer, neither can bear to be apart from one another. They might collude with one another and distrust the world/people 'out there'. They might enable one another in their pathology, perhaps encouraging one another to act out or feeding each other's habits (e.g. in overspending, over-eating or over-drinking). Another example might be the 'overly-affectionate' or the 'over-expression of admiration in public'; they are so wrapped up in one another that they are unaware or uncaring of their environment. A worst case co-

dependent dynamic might be the Bonnie and Clyde archetype!

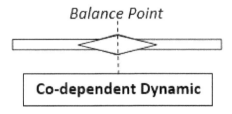

Let's Get Attached... In a balanced way!

Many years ago, Alfred Korzybski[6] wrote that "the map is not the territory." When it comes to relationships, people tend to confuse what is in their head (the map) with the outside world (the territory).

It is as if we have a mental template of other people and things and we then expect the world to *be* like our templates. This can become problematic because we might have an internal representation (mental template) of someone that is not really how that person is. We might even have a glamorised view of what a relationship *should* be like and then get disappointed when the real world doesn't live up to our internal picture.

In addition, we may attribute our happiness to our partner ("I'm only happy when I'm with you".) Whilst there is nothing wrong with associating good feelings with our loved one (indeed this positively essential!), the problem arises if we believe that our happiness *depends* on them. This would mean we cannot have happiness without our partner, leading to what we call the 'obsessive possessive': "If I'm not with you, I cannot be happy" (or the rather drastic "I can't live if living is without you").

Dependency, Needs and Unmet Needs[7]

When we mistakenly identify our happiness, security and esteem with another person, we are, in effect, placing our wellbeing in the hands of another by deferring responsibility to them. By making *them* responsible for our feelings, we make ourselves dependent on that person. Although perhaps flattering, this is a huge burden to place on another human being and also on the relationship itself.

Does this mean we should be completely independent? Should we place no value or meaning on our relationship and be totally self-sufficient for our ongoing wellbeing? Of course not, since there would be no relationship to speak of. By thinking in these terms, we would be creating a dichotomy of 'dependence' versus 'independence'.

We could make a link here between the nature of dependence/independence and the advance/retreat dynamic explored in chapter 1. Why do some people have more of a dependent/advance energy and others have more of an independent/retreat energy? In part, the answer lies in our needs and unmet needs.

Everybody has needs and some people seem needier than others. It is important to note here, however, that *retreating* energies have just as many unmet needs as *advancing*. The difference lies in the denial of needs verses the desperation of needs.

Some needs we have are here and now; for example, we might be genuinely hungry or thirsty, desire contact, want to help someone who is struggling. However, some of our needs are replays of the past. It is as if there is a part of us left behind (probably in childhood) because we experienced an unmet need (in the past) that got stored away.

Why do some unmet needs get stored away and others not? Possibly because the unmet need caused us hurt or pain at the time (physical, emotional and/or mental). Our psychological system then keeps trying to meet the need (years later) but it is never satisfied (because the original moment is long gone). In this sense, the pursuit of meeting our unmet needs is a learnt reaction. Even as an adult, if we experience rejection or hunger or a threat that is strong enough, we will most probably develop a learnt reaction to that event or person. If someone experiences a strong enough rejection or threat from someone else, they will generally seek to avoid that person and/or situation.

In order not to re-experience the hurt of unmet needs, we create psychological patterns to protect ourselves in certain situations or with certain people/types of people; these patterns are advancing or retreating:

- Someone who is an advancing/dependent energy will be trying to meet their old needs through other people/situations. The driver is: *Meet need = No more hurt*.
- Someone who uses a retreating/independent energy will be trying to suppress (or avoid feeling) old needs. The driver is: *Feel no need = No more hurt*.

In both of the patterns above, the advancing or retreating energies may also treat 'here and now' needs in the same manner. In chapter 5, we will look at some ideas for 'cleaning up the past'.

Unattached Attachment: The Interdependent Relationship

The healthiest relationships we have encountered seem to have a secure 'unattached attachment'. Both partners take responsibility for themselves, truly owning their own experience whilst taking *joint* responsibility for the relationship itself.

This 'unattached attachment' is a place of interdependence, where we can be self-sufficient whilst *choosing* to share our life experience with someone else.

Perhaps the key point of interdependence is that we *choose* to be with our partner rather than *needing* to be with them. We then let go of needing our partner to be a particular way and we let go of trying to control or change them.

An interdependent relationship appears to be based on acceptance and unconditional love; however, we can still have boundaries and express our preferences. For an advancing energy to develop interdependence, they would need to learn to express their preferences just once rather than endlessly repeating themselves. A retreating energy, on the other hand, would need to learn to speak up and express their preferences in the first place!

In interdependence, we take ownership of our internal states (emotions and thoughts) whilst being clear with our partner as to what states we are experiencing. We communicate what 'makes' us happy and what 'makes' us less than happy (without blame or self-deprecation). Our partner listens and acts accordingly (and sometimes not). If they consistently act in conflict with our boundaries and preferences, we may then have some other choices to make about the status of the relationship itself. Even here, we would first listen to what our partner has to say (e.g. why they are not prepared or able to act in accordance with our stated boundaries) and then take action accordingly.

Modelling the Interdependent Relationship

In order to model this 'ideal' relationship, it would be useful to understand what interdependence looks like. Here are some examples:

- **Interests**: the interdependent couple will have shared interests, hobbies and activities and they may also have their own personal interests. The point here is that they are aware of the ecology of their interests (i.e. they would not want their interests to impact harmfully on each other or the relationship). In addition, each partner is likely to be as happy spending time in their own company as they do in each other's.

- **Roles & strengths**: the interdependent couple know that they have their own strengths and 'development areas' and will use their strengths when taking on roles within the relationship, for example: negotiating, handling poor service, fixing things and cooking. However, they are still prepared to share ownership for these activities rather than abdicate responsibility (thus avoiding a dependency trap).

- **Communication & decision making**: both partners take responsibility for communicating and making decisions. Money is a classic example, where the couple discuss requirements, issues and actions in an adult way, rather than one being dependant on the other (or one spending without thought whilst the other 'nags' about budgets). Decisions tend to be discussed in a truly 'win/win' way with both partners seeking a fair solution.

- **Contracting**: both partners are prepared to express what their boundaries are... what is okay and what is not. What will they tolerate and what will they not tolerate? What would be a 'deal-breaker' for them? In turn, they both clearly understand their partner's boundaries.

- **Responsibility**: in the same way that the couple will take joint responsibility for decisions, each individual will be responsible for themselves. This means owning their own feelings, thoughts, opinions, needs, wants, outcomes, goals etc. It also means they *do not blame* each other for how they feel, goals not being met etc. We sometimes hear folk saying that their partner has held them back or stopped them from achieving things in life; most often we have found that this is an excuse and indeed, when they are not with their partner any longer, they will often find some other excuse for why they are not achieving things in their life.

- **Tough times**: in an interdependent relationship, each person will support their partner in times of crisis. In times of trouble they can turn to one another and they can relate to and help each other. In the words of Phil McGraw[8], they become each other's 'soft place to fall'.

So how might we reach a place of interdependence? The first stage is in letting go of the fear of 'losing' our partner. The apparent paradox is that letting go of attachment doesn't mean losing our connection, indeed it may bring us closer together. Letting go of attachment actually means letting go of our reliance on and/or compulsion about our partner. Letting go of compulsive attachment opens the door for secure attachment.

'Balancing' Exercises: Dealing with the Map and the Territory

Let us return to the idea highlighted earlier in this chapter: 'the map is not the territory'. We will be exploring lots of strategies and behaviours for healthy map and territory throughout the rest of this book. However, what do we mean when we talk about our relationship map and the relationship territory?

- **Our Relationship Map**: We carry around all sorts of 'internal pictures' and beliefs about other people (and indeed the world in general). If the internal pictures and beliefs we have about a particular person are 'healthy' then this will tend to engender a healthier relationship with that person. If, however, we carry around 'negative' internal pictures (and associations) about a person, this will tend to govern how we interact with them. It is as if we hold transparent image over the other person and use it to filter our experience of them and our interactions with them. Fortunately, our internal pictures and beliefs are malleable and can be easily changed and updated.

- **Our Relationship Territory**: In most relationships there will be moments of 'unmet needs'. No-one is completely enlightened... sometimes we all say and do things we regret. Sometimes our loved ones may say or do things we feel less than happy about too! When these things happen, we may be able to communicate them to our partner. However, there may be other things that we do *not* communicate perhaps because we are not fully aware of them or we may be scared to mention them, or perhaps we do not find the time to speak about them.

Key Pointer

The Tunnel and the Fog

We sometimes use the metaphor of an interconnecting tunnel between a couple. When all is well and communication is clean and 'up to date', the tunnel remains clear and they can truly see/experience each other.

However, significant issues, when unspoken, tend to create a layer of mist in the tunnel between them. If time goes on and issues are not resolved, the tunnel gets mistier and foggier until it is hard for them to see properly the issues between them. It also becomes harder for them to see new issues arising. They no longer really see each other anymore... just the fog. They become acclimatised to the fog (i.e. it becomes 'normal') and so they begin to drift apart from one another and communication becomes more generalised and distorted.

If fog becomes the problem, what is the solution? In one word: 'communication'. In order to keep things clear, when they notice the tunnel getting foggy, they are best served by speaking with their partner about what troubles them at the earliest opportunity. If done within the spirit of the Five Relationship Graces, this should help to clear the fog and prevent any drifting apart.

It is important that we manage both our internal and external worlds effectively. It is essential for us to maintain a healthy internal 'map' (of ourselves, our partner and the relationship), and then, clean communication handles the 'territory' aspect of our relationship.

An Interdependent Future

The nature and purpose of the interdependent relationship is to maintain balance and harmony. The interdependent couple integrate all the benefits of dependence and independence. They love as unconditionally as they can and they seek to develop themselves. They work to resolve their own unhelpful patterns and become ever more resourceful as a person and as a partner. When both people in a relationship are committed to becoming the best they can be, the need for the push-pull of dependence-independence melts away.

The interdependent couple support themselves, one another, and the relationship they share.

Chapter 3

Transforming Interactions

"To love is to admire with the heart; to admire is to love with the mind."
Theophile Gautier

In This Chapter...

In this chapter, we will be introducing the idea of constructive and destructive behaviours in relationships. We will be utilising research by John Gottman to illustrate a working model.

We will be exploring the following questions:

- What are the Four Horsemen of the Apocalypse in relationships?
- What is the difference between constructive and destructive behaviours?
- How do you know if you are behaving destructively?
- How do successful couples behave?

We have all, no doubt, seen couples treat one another well and also seen couple who treat each other not so well. How people treat and behave towards each other tends to determine the quality of their relationship (and hence the quality of their life experience). It seems counter-intuitive and rather sad from the outside, when two people who apparently love each other can behave so unpleasantly!

To help us transform our interactions, we are going to introduce some amazing research that has been carried out by a team of social psychologists. By raising our awareness of destructive behaviours, we have a better chance of spotting and hence preventing them. We will then explore some alternative *constructive* behaviours that can enhance the quality of our relationships.

The Four Horsemen of the Apocalypse

Imagine a couple as they sit and discuss an issue which has been causing friction between them. As to the content of the issue, you might add your own example here. Perhaps he isn't doing his fair share around the house. Perhaps she is spending a lot of time with her friends. In this instance, the couple are in the honeymoon phase of their relationship and what they probably don't realise is that how they go about exploring this issue will likely determine the status of their relationship in five years' time.

In an extraordinary series of studies, John Gottman and his team of social psychologists have been able to consistently predict the long-term future condition of a couple's relationship. By observing just five minutes of how the couple interact when discussing an issue, Gottman and his team have a 91% success rate at predicting whether the couple will still be together five years later.

It appears that one of the most critical factors in a successful relationship is how couples interact and handle difference (e.g. of opinion, perspective and/or personality). In his book, *Why Marriages Succeed or Fail*, Gottman[9] highlights a series of behaviours that appear when a relationship is less likely to succeed in the long term. He calls these the 'Four Horsemen of the Apocalypse' for a relationship: stonewalling, defensiveness, criticism and contempt.

1. **Stonewalling** is about *avoidance*; certain topics become off limits so we don't talk about them. This can be a mutual decision or one partner overtly refusing to discuss a "hot" topic.

2. **Defensiveness** is linked to *apprehension*; not taking responsibility and by implication wanting to blame someone

else. When we become overly defensive we may start seeing conflict where it doesn't exist and give out hostile defensive 'vibes' toward our partner based on this perception.

3. **Criticism** is about *antagonism*; attacking the other party overtly. Critical behaviours can become habitual and reflexive. The trap of criticism springs when we start to criticise even the smallest thing, for example how someone loads the dishwasher!

Defensiveness and criticism are usually two opposite but complementary sides of the same coin, where one side wants to attack and the other side parries. This is a common pattern in relationships: often one partner adopts the critical role while the other is defensive. Sometimes there is a flip-flop effect but more often roles are adopted. In the 'loading the dishwasher' example above, the defensive partner may stop an action because they know they will be criticised for 'doing it wrong'; this doesn't work of course, because then they may be criticised for 'not doing it at all'!

4. **Contempt** is about *aversion* and is considered to be the worst and most toxic of the horseman. Here we are in the realms of insults, name-calling, sarcasm, hostility and cynicism; and according to Gottman the body language of contempt includes sneering and eye rolling.

A subtler signal of contempt can be seen when examining micro-expressions such as the asymmetrical lip curl to demonstrate contempt. According to Paul Eckman[10], micro-expressions last typically less than a twenty-fifth of a second. Whilst we can learn to consciously recognise micro-expressions by improving your visual acuity, we tend to recognise micro-expressions unconsciously anyway. If our partner is regularly flashing contempt at us, we will get that at an unconscious emotional level!

If a relationship continues to exist in this state, affection and love will usually be dissolved by the acidity of contempt. To begin with, this feeling may be experienced only now and then, but each time contempt is expressed, it becomes more concentrated. Sadly, over an extended period of time, contempt can destroy love.

A Case In Point

Something I have observed in some cultures (particularly the British), is that criticism and contempt in relationship often seem to be culturally supported. I notice this most often when in a female-only group when women talk about their partners. Women often spend time criticising and putting down their partner in discussions with other women and using generalisations about men. Women who don't join in often get cold shouldered by the group or get the criticism turned on them.

This even happens in situations where the women don't know each other. I was in a women's clothes shop one day and Joe was patiently waiting while I tried things on. As I went into the changing room I said something to him which he acknowledged while busily writing in a notebook. I was okay with that and also knew he was writing something in his ideas book which I appreciate the importance of. The shop assistant rolled her eyes and said something about "typical men."

I chose not to respond and just noticed the invitation to play the game of 'kick men'. Why did she do it? My guess is that she was trying to establish rapport with me, so the intention behind the behaviour was positive. In most instances the shopper would have joined in with her out of cultural habit and rapport would have been established with the shop assistant (whilst unconsciously sabotaging their primary relationships!)

Melody

Successful Couples and the Counter Horsemen

Do successful couples argue? Of course they do! But Gottman also found that successful couples tend to have a ratio of at least five good experiences to one bad. Good experiences might include engaging interactions like hugs, cuddles, a genuine "I love you," kind words, compliments, gifts, doing things together and talking about joint interests.

In our experience, even when arguing, successful couples tend not to dredge up the past. They stay present with the situation at hand. Additionally, even in the heat of the moment, they still want to work through it and out the other side to a conclusion. This doesn't necessarily mean they spend hours processing something without a break, it simply means they prefer not to 'hang on to old stuff'.

Something that Gottman alludes to but does not pull together into a model (like the 'Four Horsemen') is the positive spin. What is the model for successful couples? How do *they* handle difference?

According to Steve Andreas[11], "Fritz Perls used to say that: 'Contact is the appreciation of differences' – in contrast to seeing differences as bad." In our own workshops, we have introduced the four *counter-horsemen* of awareness, acceptance, appreciation and admiration. As well as providing a direct counter for each of Gottman's horsemen, there are 'levels' that couples transcend as they face and resolve their differences.

1. **Awareness**: The first level, *awareness* is about acknowledging that there is an issue and being prepared to discuss it rather than avoiding it. Stonewalling (or avoidance) often arises either when differences of opinion emerge or when we don't understand each other's interests. In some cases, we have become disenchanted with the very thing that we thought was 'cute' about our partner at the beginning of the relationship.

Awareness is the counter to stonewalling. We need to notice if distance is creeping in, particularly where we feel as if we are withdrawing from each other. It is important to recognise and acknowledge difference and to engage in dialogue. By attempting to understand one another we are less likely to disengage further.

2. **Acceptance**: The second horseman is defensiveness and this is countered with the second level, *acceptance*. A key element is staying open and listening to one another. By listening we stay connected and we can then be open to the concept of difference being okay. If difference is okay, defensiveness is unnecessary. A*cceptance* is about staying open to our partner's perspective and knowing that it is more productive to listen than it is to get defensive.

3. **Appreciation**: The third horseman, criticism is perhaps almost as poisonous as contempt, particularly if it has become a habit and automatic. To counter criticism, we need to stay alert and search out ways to appreciate each other. Not only is difference okay, it is also useful. We need a change of mind-set where we can truly appreciate the uniqueness of our partner as the gift it really is.

This third level, *appreciation,* is about valuing the fact that our partner can be and do different things to us and instead of criticising them, we understanding that this is useful to the relationship. We may even praise the fact that they do certain things better than we do ourselves.

In our marriage, one thing I appreciate about Joe is his playfulness (we've been married since 1994). He is constantly changing his accent and being quite silly. This still makes me laugh and is something I can both accept and appreciate about him. Joe has often commented that he is surprised that I don't get annoyed by his behaviours. It was talking about things like this that enabled us to come up with our *Counter Horseman*. We realised that in many other couples we had seen small things like making silly voices or noises become a source of contempt.

Melody

Often when we scratch the surface of relationships that have soured, we find that the rot has set in over small, very unimportant differences that have then become inflamed. By taking notice of these small differences and changing our perspective, we have the opportunity to safeguard our relationships. If small things stay small, bigger issues are less likely to arise... and if they do, there is a clearer path to seeking (and finding) a resolution.

4. **Admiration**: Relationship breakdown is rarely a sudden event, almost always it is a gradual escalation of lost respect, love and admiration; as love diminishes, contempt grows.

The final level, *admiration*, is where we see our difference as a part of relationship excellence. We seek to find integration between opposing positions and to create synergy rather than contempt. Instead of dropping into hurtful conflict, we get inspired to innovate.

In *The Seven Principles for Making Marriage Work*, Gottman[12] suggests that: "fondness and admiration are antidotes for contempt. If you maintain a sense of respect for your spouse, you are less likely to act disgusted with him or her when you disagree. So, fondness and admiration prevent the couple from being trounced by the four horsemen."

> **Key Pointer**
>
> When was the last time you openly and overtly expressed your admiration of (and to) your partner? Do you tell others what you most admire about your partner? Do you take pride in their accomplishments?
>
> Make a point every day to tell your partner what you appreciate and admire about them. As you do this notice how much more loving and secure your relationship becomes.

The Interaction Scale

Below, we have numbered each 'horseman' on a scale of -4 to +4 to give a sense of 'layers' of toxicity (minus scores) to layers of healthiness (plus scores).

The following table gives you some examples of what each layer looks like:

DESTRUCTIVE		CONSTRUCTIVE	
Gottman's Horseman	**Behaviours**	**The Counter Horsemen**	**Behaviours**
Contempt (*Aversion*) -4	• Eye rolling • Sarcasm • Insults • Spiteful comments	Admiration +4	• Show interest & respect • Encourage & extol virtues

			• Give compliments
Criticism (*Antagonism*) -3	• Criticising • Attacking • Generalising (e.g. you always/ never) • Irritable with partner	Appreciation +3	• Feedback & praise • Show support • Kind and patient with partner
Defensiveness (*Apprehension*) -2	• Making excuses • Defending oneself • Countering (yes, but) • 'Walking on egg shells'	Acceptance +2	• Stay open • Listen • Show empathy • See things from partner's perspective • Acknowledge own mistakes
Stonewalling (*Avoidance*) -1	• Topics become 'off limits' • Changing subject • Withdrawing and ignoring	Awareness +1	• Engage in dialogue • Acknowledge difference

How do you know which level you are at?

The reality is, we may be at different levels for different things. We might, for example, hate the way our partner snores, but love the way they ask us if we want a coffee when they are making one for themselves!

Here are three 'audits' you can do for yourself to get you thinking:

Interaction Audit (Part 1)

Consider a list of topics that you tend to discuss (or avoid) in your relationship. What do you have conversations about, particularly practical things?

Be honest with yourself and score each of the following topic areas listed below on a scale from -4 to +4 (using the *Interaction Scale*). Feel free to add other topics and to write a more specific list within each topic (e.g. breaking housework down into things like: cleaning, washing-up, loading/unloading dishwasher, dusting, gardening etc.).

How do you communicate (and how *well* do you communicate) about:

- Family (own and partner's)?
- Children/child rearing?
- Friends (own and partner's)?
- Money/finance?
- Sex?
- Roles in relationship?
- Sharing tasks (e.g. cooking)?
- Work?
- Housework?

Interaction Audit (Part 2)

Look at each of the Horsemen and Counter-horsemen in turn (from -4 through to +4 on the *Interaction Scale*). Where might you exhibit some of these behaviours towards your partner? What specific topics (and sub-topics) might you sometimes feel contempt regarding your partner; then what might you criticise? What do you get defensive about? What do you avoid talking about or doing? What topics do you acknowledge regarding your partner (e.g. that they have done something)? What do you accept (even if it not your way of doing things)? What topics do you appreciate (e.g. saying thank you)? What do you admire your partner for (and how do you express that)?

Communication Audit

Consider the following questions, both from a destructive and constructive perspective. In what *ways* (e.g. respectful or disrespectful) might you communicate? And *about what* might you criticise or praise your partner?

1. How do you talk to your partner when you are with others?
2. How do you talk to your partner when you are *not* with others (i.e. you are alone together)?
3. How do you talk about your partner to others when your partner is with you?
4. How do you talk about your partner to others when your partner is *not* with you?

It is interesting to note that in some relationships, couples can be critical (*destructive*) *towards* one another but then talk to others *about* one another (in their absence) in appreciative terms (*constructive*). Alternatively, some couples talk to each other in constructive terms but then disrespectfully when talking to others in their absence. These incongruent forms of communication may raise questions about the health of the relationship.

Chapter 4

Becoming 'Balanced-Constructive'

"Love is… a daily balancing act!"

Kim Casali

In This Chapter...

In this chapter, we will be integrating what we have covered so far into a workable model. This will help you to identify healthy and unhealthy behaviours in relationships, both in yourself and in others. We will also introduce some practical tips on how to remain 'balanced-constructive', even when your partner is not!

We will be exploring the following questions:

- What is balanced-constructive behaviour?
- What leads to unbalanced and destructive behaviours?
- What are some examples of destructive and constructive?
- How can we remain balanced-constructive?

In Summary

So far, we have explored two models that describe and explain some of the healthy and unhealthy behaviours within relationships. In this chapter, we will combine these models to give us a fuller picture. It will also give us some ideas as to how we can become healthier and interact more healthily in any relationship.

1) Balanced/Unbalanced

In the previous chapters we introduced the 'relationship dynamic' model of advance/retreat. If we now think of the dynamic as a *continuum* we have the following:

ADVANCE $\longleftrightarrow$ RETREAT

At extremes, we might consider an individual's 'energy' as unbalanced. The advancing energy can seem invasive, suffocating and smothering. The retreating energy comes across as absent, unavailable and perhaps unapproachable.

2) Constructive/Destructive

As discussed in the previous chapter, when engaging and interacting with our partner, we will have tendencies towards constructive or destructive behaviours. Some behaviours will be more extreme than others and may change depending on the context. For most couples, the time they are more likely to resort to destructive approaches will be when they feel stressed, under pressure or under threat. Of course, some people appear to have 'learnt' destructive behaviours through socialisation; perhaps they grew up in a psychologically unhealthy environment (e.g. parents arguing/abusive) and don't understand another way of being.

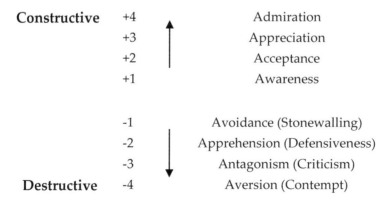

Constructive	+4		Admiration
	+3		Appreciation
	+2		Acceptance
	+1		Awareness
	−1		Avoidance (Stonewalling)
	−2		Apprehension (Defensiveness)
	−3		Antagonism (Criticism)
Destructive	−4		Aversion (Contempt)

The above is an overview of the layers (or levels) of how couples treat each other, both constructively and destructively. This model on its own is useful but doesn't tell the whole story. For example:

- What if a couple admire each other and yet one partner expresses this constantly whereas the other feels it but does not express it? This would still be unbalanced and hence seems unhealthy.
- Alternatively, we might imagine a couple who are constantly expressing how wonderful the other is to the point where it becomes sickening to others: in this sense, the 'over-expression' of both partners could still be considered pathological and obsessive.
- Another constructive but unbalanced behaviour might be the person who sings the praises of their loved one to others but not directly to their partner.

Balanced AND Constructive: The Relationship Dynamics Model

By combining the two models, we begin to see something that could describe the difference between the healthy and unhealthy aspects of a relationship:

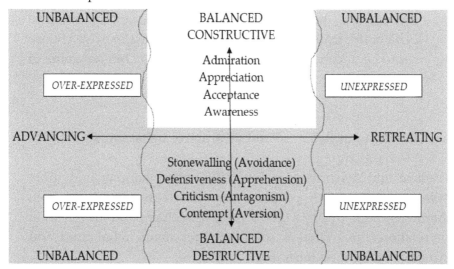

43

A colleague of ours, Pete Farthing, suggested that the clear area in the model is 'love based' and the grey area is more likely 'fear based'. This put us in mind of the difference between 'conditional' and 'unconditional' love. The grey area would be conditional and the clear area would tend to be more unconditional.

- **Conditional love** (i.e. "I love you *if…*" or "I'll love you *if and only if…*") relies on our partner being the way we want them to be; and in this sense it is controlling (and hence probably fear based).
- **Unconditional love** (i.e. "I love you just as you are" or "I love you for being you") does not rely on our partner being a particular way or to change/be different to how (and who) they are. Indeed, unconditional love means totally accepting everything about your partner. And here, acceptance does not just mean 'tolerating', it means accepting as if being given a wonderful gift! Can we be 'unconditional' all the time? Probably not, as to do this would be akin to being spiritually enlightened! Even if we can develop a generally unconditional temperament (personality), our thoughts and feelings will still be affected by our moods and there will be contexts where we might find it less-than-easy to stay enlightened (e.g. destructive behaviours from our partner). Indeed, we would **not** recommend accepting harmful behaviours from our partner. There may be times we choose *not* to be unconditional; we can love a *person* but not some of their *behaviours*.

What can lead to unbalanced and destructive behaviours?

If *balanced* and *constructive* is healthier, easier, happier and more fulfilling, why would people want to create stress, tension, disharmony, pain, upset, anger, worry, resentment and bitterness in their relationships? What is so compelling about unbalanced and destructive thought patterns and behaviours?

Here is a summary (though not necessarily an exhaustive list) of why people may resort to unbalanced and destructive behaviours:

- They grew up in an unhealthy environment and so this is their default template (and as a result they do not have alternative strategies). Of course, this doesn't have to be a template for life. Plenty of people have grown up in hostile and unhappy environments but have learnt how to develop healthy relationships later in life. The next chapter will give you some ideas on how to *balance* yourself and develop a more *constructive* mindset.
- Needs are not being met in the present moment. These could be 'historical' needs (i.e. old needs that were not met in childhood) or 'present' needs (i.e. is actually related to something that is happening in the current moment). Historical unmet needs tend to create a more extreme internal reaction in us (often quite childlike), whereas a present unmet need is more momentary.
  - o Historical needs: These could be 'historical' needs that are re-triggered/restimulated in the present moment. (What we mean is that a present-day behaviour/ trigger stimulates a hurt that was created in childhood.) Perhaps our partner doesn't make us a cup of tea when they make themselves one and we feel deeply hurt, as if they obviously don't love us anymore (and this feels like evidence supporting the old hurt).
  - o Present needs: Things may happen 'in the now' where we feel, for example, put down or ignored by our partner. Whether they mean to do this or not, we might feel angry in the moment but it passes quickly. If the feeling lingers, it is more likely to be a historical need not being met.
- Active retriggering of old hurts. This may be another way of talking about historical unmet needs but we often react when

'old stuff' is restimulated. Times in the past where we have felt hurt, fearful and/or angry can be set off by new events. For example, a particular behaviour, look, phrase or tone of voice used by our partner may remind us of somethings said/done by one of our parents (or siblings or teachers etc). We regress immediately and react.

Destructive Associations in Relationships

The nature of emotional reactions being learnt and retriggered is also known as '*anchoring*'. Anchoring[13] is a term used in the field of neuro-linguistic programming for a naturally occurring phenomenon. It happens when two things become linked in the brain. The links can be something we see, hear, feel, smell or taste. For example, many of us have songs that we associate with a relationship. The song starts to play on the radio and suddenly we experience a feeling about that relationship. Hopefully that will be a warm fuzzy feeling, however sometimes we have negative anchors that trigger less pleasant emotions (e.g. a song that reminds us of a painful breakup).

Some anchors are very obvious. If we experience fear when we see or hear something, the likelihood is we will form an association. Later, if we see or hear something similar, we re-experience the fear, even if it is irrational in the new situation. In general terms, this is a survival strategy, i.e. avoiding those things that caused us fear or pain in the past! Anchoring can also have a subtler and unexpected impact on a relationship both positively and negatively.

The stimulation of this feeling is automatic once in place. Positive relationship anchors strengthen a relationship while negative ones weaken it. Many of these anchors are outside of our conscious awareness so we may not realise the impact they are having.

A Case In Point

Anthony Robbins talks about an example of a negative anchor on one his audio programmes. In this example he talks about what happens when a husband is experiencing problems and stress at work.

Every day he leaves work feeling angry and unhappy. While feeling this feeling he walks through the front door of his home and the first thing he sees is his wife's face. Unknowingly this creates an anchor that becomes triggered by the sight of his wife's face. This experience is replicated day after day the anchor becomes very strong.

What happens next is where the problem really begins. Imagine the scene, the husband has a good day, he is feeling good and he walks through his front door. What happens? He sees his wife and then feels bad. He doesn't know why.

Fast forward after repeated experiences of negative feelings being triggered by the sight of his wife the husband is now starting to think he might not love his wife anymore. What is so sad here is that the issue is not the marriage (assuming there are no other relationship tensions).

Consider how often this must happen in relationships, where people are having unpleasant experiences in their lives that accidentally get associated with their marriage and their partner.

Anchors can be sudden. Consider a couple having their first baby. If the baby being born is a 'shock' to the relationship, it can act like a dramatic (or even traumatic) event; the couple do not see each other in the same way anymore. Alternatively, it could be a 'positive' drama that brings them together, a closer unit.

Anchors can also form gradually over time. Have you ever heard of someone taking work-stress home with them? We have both coached individuals who have been under pressure at work. When they get home, their kids run over to them excitedly and jump on them, wanting their attention… whilst their partner wants to talk about their day. And so, the individual ends up feeling stressed at home too.

<u>So how do we counter these 'negative anchors'?</u>

The first step is understanding how and where negative anchors get set up and then recognising when one is happening in your relationship. If you consider now any 'less-than-positive' feelings you might have about your partner... is it really about them or is it about a negative anchor/association that has been set up? Have they actually done something specific to warrant a necessary upset or sense of distrust?

Alternatively, is this upset the triggering of an old anchor? Is it really your partner's face you see when you feel upset or angry with them?

The trick here is to recognise the difference between (a) an accidental negative anchor being set up, (b) the triggering of 'old stuff' (which may have nothing to do with them) or (c) if they have actually behaved in a fashion that goes beyond your boundaries of what is acceptable.

From here, the most important step is *self-awareness*. We need to stay conscious of our emotions and what is causing them. We need to own our feelings and manage our state before we engage with our partner. This way we can share our problems with our partner and avoid inappropriately transferring the issue to the relationship.

In addition to this, we need to make a point of creating positive anchors in our relationships, i.e. about our partner and our lives together. By creating strong positive anchors, we are also putting in a safeguard to protect against accidental negative triggers.

A Case In Point

To the outside world, an issue can seem trivial, but to the individual they can become distorted and exaggerated. One woman reported that her husband regularly did the washing up and when she went into the kitchen, all she noticed was how the tea-towel was not hung up straight! She would then 'tut' and complain.

As she developed some self-awareness (through coaching and personal development workshops), she made a decision to thank her husband for washing up (not because he was 'helping her to do housework' but because she felt it was good to appreciate each other). She would then quietly straighten the tea-towel because she preferred it to be straight.

She realised that it is okay to have standards and values (e.g. about tidiness), however, when her standards were too rigid, she would tend to experience more unhappiness.

Perhaps her next step (if she so chose) would be to notice how she could let go of caring if the towel was straight or not!

Melody

Can anchors simply disappear over time?

Some associations can weaken over time if they are not restimulated. In addition, we can also become desensitised to some of the associations we have (known as 'habituation'). If a couple have been together for some time, it is all too easy to begin to take each other for granted. What used to feel loving, now becomes background. We see each other every day but we don't really notice each other. Even the words "I love you," whilst usually constructive, can become white noise and said without a true *'gaze-into-each-others-eyes-and-really-mean-it'*. This is where the anchor is becoming 'worn-out' and no longer elicits a significant response. Whilst this may be useful for the slow erasure of mild negative anchors, it is not conducive to a long-term, *fulfilling* relationship. We will discuss ideas for restoring and re-engaging a fulfilling relationship in the final chapter.

Examples of behaviours

Destructive behaviours are those that are designed (or have the effect) to hurt or put someone down. Constructive behaviours are those that help to build or maintain someone's self-esteem and wellbeing.

Destructive Behaviours	Constructive Behaviours
• Shouting at • Verbal/physical abuse • Name calling • Threatening • Public humiliation (e.g. telling others what they dislike about their partner) • Put downs, direct sarcasm, humour at the expense of • Lying, stealing • Infidelity, cheating, sexually charged flirting with others • Persistently argumentative and antagonistic, spoiling for a fight • Ignoring, not listening • Talking over • Expecting them to take all the responsibility (e.g. do *all* the cooking/ housework/ childcare)	• Engaging in conversation, listening, showing interest • Complimenting • Complementary teasing (i.e. both find it humorous and the teasing goes both ways) • Respecting • Remaining loyal/ faithful • Speaking one's truth with kindness • Giving gifts • Speaking in a 'soft' tonality • Offering support • Laughing with and being playful together • Sharing interests • Engaging in joint activities • Telling stories together • Reminiscing about good times

Remaining 'Balanced Constructive'

For most human beings, it is challenging to remain 'balanced-constructive' all the time. Indeed, it can certainly be less than easy to stay 'self-actualised' when faced with an unbalanced and/or destructive behaviour from your partner. To remain balanced and constructive when others are not, is like channelling the spirit of Gandhi! The 'trick' is to remain calm and empathetic even when someone is not giving you the same courtesy.

As a note of warning, we are *not* advocating staying in a highly destructive, unbalanced or aggressive relationship. Constant or regular verbal abuse or physical aggression does *not* a relationship make. Indeed, here in this chapter, we are looking at how to remain balanced-constructive when you are safe and generally happy in your relationship. If you do not feel safe or you are generally unhappy in your relationship then we would recommend therapeutic measures (i.e. seek professional help). We will be exploring more about your 'boundaries' in a later chapter.

How can you remain balanced and constructive when faced with destructive and/or unbalanced behaviours from your partner? For example, how might you behave if your partner is angry and lashes out at you verbally, accusing you of something you do not feel is warranted? And perhaps just as importantly, what if their anger with you *is* justified but they lash out at you when expressing how they feel?

Might you react back… give as good as you get, accuse them of something (e.g. blowing things out of proportion), get upset and/or walk away, sneer at them because this is 'typical of them' or tell them they obviously do not love you anymore? Of course, these would all be examples of destructive or unbalanced reactions.

How can we respond (which implies some *thought* process instead of reactivating mechanically) when faced with a challenge? Most methods of handling difficult behaviour in others requires staying empathetic to that person. Not always easy perhaps, but empathy dissolves anger: first your own and then the other person's. Here are some ideas for staying in empathy when faced with someone else's destructive behaviour:

1) Remember that anger is often a cover for fear. Ask yourself: "what are they frightened about right now?"

> Key Pointer
>
> **Empathy dissolves anger!**

2) Be aware that they are acting out because they are hurting in some way. Hurt tends to underlie our fear and our anger. Remind yourself that the emotional hurt they feel is like a physical pain.

3) Remind yourself that it may not be about you. It may not really be your face they are seeing right now, but an internal representation, a memory, a ghost from the past. You are merely triggering an old pattern from their history.

4) See them as a little child (scared, in pain or simply naïve) but without belittling them. You are seeing through their mask to the hurt child within. Ask yourself: "What do they need right now?"

5) Remember that a difficult person is a person in difficulty. We can all be difficult sometimes. You are more likely to want to help and love a 'person in difficulty' than you are a 'difficult person'!

6) Consider the context. What has happened to them to make them act this way? What would cause *you* to act in the same manner? What must they have been through?

7) Remember that you are both on the same side. Whatever is going on 'out there', you are stronger facing it together rather than divided.

And here are some behaviours you might find effective:

1) If they are angry, acknowledge the anger… label it: "you seem angry right now". Even if that seems obvious (and even if they continue reacting angrily "of course I'm angry"), the act of acknowledging and labelling a feeling is the first step in resolving it.
2) Ask: "what's happened?" Give them a chance to express their anger in a more useful manner by expressing what they are angry *about*. Be prepared to ask for more information.
3) Ask them: "what do you need?" Listen to what they say. Can you then meet those needs or do they simply need help or space to solve the situation for themselves?

A note on delivery style here: we can say the same words in a variety of ways and get different responses. Ensure that your tone is warm and clear. Avoid sounding parental or patronising as this may escalate the situation, no matter what words you use.

If you can maintain a state of empathy, you will remember more easily the things you accept, appreciate and admire in your partner. By responding with love rather than reacting with a counter-attack, you will help them more quickly to dissolve their anger and bring them back to a constructive frame.

Throughout your endeavour to remain 'Balanced-Constructive', remember the third of the Five Relationship Graces:

> *We will act constructively towards one another, particularly when it comes to our differences. We will speak respectfully about one another when we are with others.*

Chapter 5

The Readiness Factor

(Preparing yourself for a Balanced-constructive Relationship)

"Be the person your dog already thinks you are."

Anon

In This Chapter...

In this chapter, we will help you to find you *own* balance, to get into a state of readiness for your ideal relationship! This chapter is all about *you* and *your* side of the deal. Whether you are in relationship or not, the first part of the chapter will be 100% relevant to you. Do not under-estimate the power of self-awareness; understanding yourself is a critical factor in any loving partnership. The second part will then be particularly useful if you are wanting to create a new dance partner in your life.

We will be exploring the following questions:

- How can you become ready for the relationship you want?
- How can you find your own 'balance point'?
- How might you develop a more constructive approach?
- What can you do to 'clean-up' old, unhealthy patterns?
- What can you do to find your perfect partner?

Part One: Being the best version of you

If it takes two to tango, how can you get yourself dance fit... fit for a **balanced-constructive** relationship?

If you are already in relationship, the first step to a healthy transformation is for *you* to become the improvements you want to experience with your partner. If you are currently single, then prepare yourself to become the person that your dream partner will fall in love with!

By becoming the best version of you, you also become the *healthiest* version of you. It is difficult for a partner to be unhealthy with you if you have developed and become more balanced. We were once taught a metaphor of two people pushing and struggling against one another[14]. If one person stands up, the other person has two options… stand up as well and become more balanced or continue trying to push against zero-resistance… and hence fall over. Of course, we are not doing this to make our partner fall over, instead we are 'stepping back' to create a space for them to become balanced too.

a) <u>Handling 'unbalanced-destructive' societal norms</u>

Society, the media and pop science tell us that men and women are from different planets. If we are to believe a popular book title, then apparently men are from Mars and women are from Venus[15]! The stereotypes we read about sometimes border on the realms of sexism (and indeed may contribute to the continuance of sexism in society and the workplace) and seem designed to perpetuate the belief that men and women should oppose and ridicule each other.

When couples buy into the stereotypes portrayed by society, we often see one partner 'parenting' the other. It appears to be their 'job' to be mother/father, e.g. telling their partner off, buying clothes for them (i.e. dressing them), managing finances, stating opinions on behalf of their partner, apologising on their behalf and controlling/tempering them. This may of course work for many couples, but does it seem balanced? Parenting in partnerships would tend to be an example of an **advancing** energy. The notion of one partner 'parenting' the other is very different from both partners agreeing to split tasks and play to their strengths.

Stereotypes are rife and they are divisive, maintaining a deep and unhealthy rift between couples. So, rather than the dull proclamations that 'men are…' and 'women are…', what about we say that there are masculine and feminine traits. On average, men have more masculine traits and women have more feminine traits. However, the reality is that we all have some masculine and some feminine traits. This gets us away from some of the unhelpful and destructive conventions. We are not suggesting 'degenderising' men and women… we are simply seeking to celebrate the similarities and differences rather than maintain a negative set of stereotypes.

Stereotypes, beliefs, metaphors and values

Culture is stacked with metaphors and stereotypes about relationships. Which societal norms do you subscribe to? Which are true for you? Which are you affected by? What is your 'relationship to relationships' and what set of beliefs do you hold? What are some of the phrases and thoughts that you sometimes voice about relationships... even in jest? Some of these beliefs may have come from your family and may be in the form of metaphors. Are these phrases empowering and constructive or limiting and destructive? If you find that some of your attitudes, beliefs and metaphors are less than positive, what might be a more useful replacement? For example:

Limiting Metaphors	Empowering Metaphors
• Ball and chain, trouble and strife. • Seven-year itch. • Under the thumb.	• A match made in heaven. • Love birds, 'lovey dovey'. • Two hearts beat as one. • In harmony.

Limiting Beliefs	Empowering Beliefs
• Relationships are never easy. • A good man/woman is hard to find. • People leave. • Treat them mean to keep them keen!	• The majority of people are in relationships. • There is someone for everyone. • Communication is the key to relationships.

To break free of some of the limiting beliefs you might have around relationships, the first step is self-awareness. To help you understand some of your own beliefs and metaphors, answer the questions below and see where the answers take you. Be as truthful and honest with yourself as you are able. It is okay to have conflicting beliefs, perhaps some helpful *and* some less so. Remember, these are things that may be true for you personally (even if they are not true for others).

We recommend you write your answers in the form of a narrative (i.e. flow of thoughts) without editing. If you are unsure about your answer to any of the following questions, write out the question and then pause. Jot down whatever pops into your head. When you re-read your narrative, underline statements that imply facts about men, women, yourself and relationships.

Beliefs:
- What is true about relationships?
- What is true about men?
- What is true about women?
- What is true about men and women?
- What is true about yourself in relationships?
- What is true about your current partner (if applicable)?
- What is true about previous partners (if applicable)?

Metaphors
- What is a relationship like?
- What are men like?
- What are women like?

- What are men and women like when together?
- You in relationship – what is that like?

Notice in your answers where there are empowering beliefs/ metaphors and where there are limiting beliefs/metaphors. Consider what some of the metaphors might mean to you and consider what impact these beliefs might have on your relationships, your state of mind and your wellbeing.

In terms of handling limiting beliefs, here are a couple of ideas:

- Ask yourself some challenging questions. In what way does this belief help me? What benefit does it bring to me? What do I gain by having that belief? Whatever answer you get to these questions, consider, can you get the benefit of the belief in a healthier way whilst purposefully letting go of that belief? For example, if someone believed that potential partners can't be trusted, perhaps the 'gain' is self-protection and avoidance of future pain. Is it possible to protect one-self *and* believe that people *can* be trusted? Of course. Even if it means staying aware of signs and signals in others whilst developing trust over time; some element of caution may be prudent when we first meet someone. Then as we get to know them, trust develops and strengthens.
- Examine a limiting belief. Is it possible that you might be using that belief as an excuse to do or not to do something? We often hear stories where a disgruntled individual complains that their partner has stopped them from: doing something, having something, travelling somewhere or succeeding in general. We also hear phrases like: "If it wasn't for my partner… (e.g. the house would be tidy)". Ironically, we have seen couples split up because of these kind of complaints… and then they still don't travel or do the thing they apparently wanted… and their house is still untidy! Of course, this is not true of all parting couples and some people do indeed do the things they wanted to do. But check this out

with yourself… is it an excuse? And what if it were possible to do the things you want to do whilst still being in a relationship?! What if a couple actually helped each other to succeed?

- Check your evidence criteria. How do/did you know the belief was true? What is/was your evidence? Now look for examples that counter your evidence. If you cannot find that counter-evidence in your own life, look for it in other people's.

When it comes to the metaphors of relationship, we sometimes refer to the 'relationship game'. So, from your perspective, if it were a game, what would it be and why? And what are the rules? On workshops we have run, there have been some really interesting answers… hide and seek, snakes and ladders, chess, rugby…

The point with eliciting your own metaphors is to then see what could be empowering/constructive and what could be limiting/destructive. Hide and seek can be good fun when both partners are playing and they know there is a place to find one another, however, it can be infuriating and lonely sometimes if you cannot find your partner!

Another aspect to get clear about is your **value** system. Where beliefs are 'what is true for you?', values are 'what is important to you?' Values tend to be context dependent and can change over time. The way to elicit your relationship values is to ask yourself: "What is important to me about relationships?" Write down at least ten things, asking each time: "and what else?" Then put the different things you have written in order of most important to least important. This is your current 'hierarchy of relationship values'.

We will pick up on beliefs and values again in the next chapter, where we look at sharing these details with a partner as a way of bonding and 'contracting' with one another.

b) <u>Finding your own balance point</u>

Imagine that your partner says they want to go away for the weekend on their own or with friends. What would be your reaction to this? Might you feel alarm, hurt, nervousness? Or at the other end of the spectrum, relief or even delight? Are you wondering why they want to go without you or are you thinking of all the things you might do whilst they are away? Or do you feel genuinely fine with them going away?

In the scenario above, it is interesting to notice not just your reaction, but also the 'emotional load' or energy behind the reaction. Some may have a mild reaction and others may have a stronger one.

The example here may give you an idea as to whether you are more of an advancing energy or retreating. To desire that your partner remain with you or you with them would be an advancing energy; so too would jealousy or unhappiness. On the other hand, to feel relief that you will get some time and space to yourself would indicate a more withdrawing energy. The degree to which you react can be anywhere on the continuum of relief/joy to fear/anger/jealousy. The balance would be a relaxed, comfortable mid-way point.

Consider for a moment, where in a relationship might you advance and where might you retreat? Alternatively, where are you relaxed and balanced?

A useful 'self-awareness' connection here is in understanding and handling your emotions. Which emotions and feelings do you tend to do more of and which do you do less of? And which do you do a lot? For example:

Anger	Love and connection
Irritation	Happiness and laughter
Jealousy	Curiosity and interest
Fear	Relaxation
Anxiety and worry	Easy confidence
Resentment	Contentment
Shame and embarrassment	Secure

If you are leaning towards the left column, have a think about what situations or triggers might stimulate those emotions. What are your 'flashpoints'? How might you handle these? If we take jealousy as an example, has your partner given you *real-world* evidence that they are not to be trusted (e.g. had an affair)? Do they flirt with others and is that flirting an invitation for sexual interaction or is it more an invitation to play (i.e. what we might call 'charm')? The point here is to step back and look at the situation from an observer position. Do you really fear that you will lose them in these situations or do you feel irritated that their attention is not on you at that moment? Of course, your answer might be none of the above!

It may be helpful here to introduce the concept of the 'self-fulfilling prophecy' (where we create the very thing we believe will happen). The very behaviour we fear our partner doing can sometimes be created by *our own* behaviour.

A Case In Point

Imagine a scenario where Fred gets irritated when Daphne does not tell him if she needs to work late. On the surface, this may seem unreasonable of her. However, if in the past, Fred reacted angrily to Daphne telling him that she had to work late, she may decide to avoid some of the hassle by not telling him up front.

If certain behaviours trigger certain reactions in you, the first step is to determine how 'real' your interpretation is. Do your concerns consistently turn out to be correct? Or are you still waiting for the possibility that your partner might do something to intentionally hurt you? Is this a feeling you have experienced before in previous relationships (i.e. is this a pattern for you)? This is known as 'reality checking'.

Be aware that it may be unreasonable to expect your partner to do/not do certain things to 'pander' to your neurosis. We **do need** to deal with any neurosis that might limit or hurt our partner (or ourselves) in some way.

One way to handle 'historical' emotions and hurts is to write them down. Get a journal and write what happened and how you felt. If appropriate, you might add what constructive and healthy things you might have done differently in preventing that situation and in handling it. One of the benefits of 'journaling' is that it helps to get it *out* of your system and for you to become more objective to it. This, in turn, helps to create a bit of distance from it and hence can help it feel less 'raw'.

The second step in handling your reactions, if you still believe that your partner may carry out your fears, is to consider your boundaries. What behaviours will you accept in a partner and what will you not tolerate? What actions would spell the end of a relationship for you? We will discuss this further in the next chapter.

Know what upsets you 'unreasonably' as well as reasonably. If both partners understand that certain triggers result in certain reactions, they can more easily manage and accept one another.

c) <u>Developing constructive approaches</u>

<u>*Self Esteem*</u>

Our psychological health is directly connected to our self-esteem. Before we move on, however, let us look at what that means.

Consider for a moment a person with very high self-esteem. How do you imagine them? Arrogant and unbearable? Or humble and wonderful? The dictionary definition of self-esteem is directed at our own personal self-regard (i.e. how we value our 'self'). This is not a helpful definition! If you ask most people: "Would you like more self-esteem?" the answer is "yes". However, if having more self-esteem takes us towards unbearable arrogance, why would we want it?

It is time to redefine self-esteem! Unbearable arrogance is not a function of high self-esteem! The reality of high self-esteem is someone who has humility, kindness, empathy and confidence to speak their mind on subjects that are important to them. They are good at asking for what they want, but never at the cost of others. This is true self-esteem! Indeed, the definition we use is: "Having a high positive regard for yourself **and** for others; valuing all life equally." We enhance our self-esteem **not** at the expense of others, but whilst enhancing their self-esteem and wellbeing *at the same time*. In this sense, the keys to true self-esteem are 'expression' and 'empathy'. One of the most productive ways of enhancing your self-esteem is to *express your truth (needs, opinions, expectations) with kindness*. This might also be called 'being assertive'. For example:

- Say no when you *need* to say no, but help the other person in some way *if you can*.
- Ask for what you want, be clear and specific - whilst being prepared for the other person's right to say no.
- Be prepared to say what you think whilst acknowledging that it is your opinion and not the truth. Listen to other people's opinions in the same way you would like them listen to yours.

It is important to note that destructive behaviours towards our partner or ourselves (e.g. belittling or putting our partner down) are signs of low self-esteem. Such behaviours tend to be used by a person to raise themselves above someone else or make themselves feel better. It is clear however, that degrading someone else actually erodes our own self-esteem (and possibly theirs as well).

On the other hand, feeling good about yourself (i.e. comfortable in your own skin), is a sign of healthy self-esteem and is the basis of confidence. Have you ever considered that 'balanced confidence' can be a very attractive quality?

d) <u>Cleaning up old patterns</u>

<u>*Creating the space – Dousing old flames*</u>

Previous partners may be viewed as angelic, demonic or perhaps a bit of both. So, what happens when someone is looking for a new partner whilst holding on to the baggage of previous relationships? Some people use the hurts from previous relationships to create an unconscious avoidance filter, seeing only what is wrong with new prospective partners they meet. Of course, this distrust is probably a protective mechanism, a method for not being hurt again.

There are also times when people hold on to a 'perfect' representation of a former lover (or object of their unrequited affection). The internal mythology of that lover may become distorted to the point of a fantasy and then they use this as a measuring stick as they meet new people. No real person can live up to that level of perfection.

There are a range of processes that can help someone to let go of past flames[16]. For example, Lucas Derks[17] has carried out years of research into what he calls 'Social Panoramas', which explores *how* and *where* we store other people in our internal map. When you think of a loved one, where are they in relationship to you in your internal world? Many people hold loved ones close and slightly to the left. If someone is seeking a relationship but already has a previous partner in the 'loved one' spot, there is no room for anyone new. Where do you store people who are 'long ago history'? If you find you have an old flame in the 'loved-one' spot, imagine pushing them into the 'long-ago history' spot, usually in the distance and over to the right or behind you.

In order to move on and grow, we need to learn from previous relationships. By jumping straight from one relationship to another, we risk taking the same old baggage and problems from one place to the next. In order to learn, we may need to take a little time for reflection. If we can consider previous relationships as 'learning experiences' for the future, what positive, constructive lessons can we take forward? Where there was hurt from a previous relationship (including parental), rather than using this to shut down, it is more productive to face these things, learn and move on. Here are some questions to help you grow through previous destructive relationships:

1. What characteristics/qualities did you find unpleasant or hurtful in the previous partner? (For this exercise, avoid writing paragraphs of what happened. Stick to key words that label the behaviour, e.g. 'disrespectful'.)

2. For each quality, what do/did you learn from having that experience in your life? And what resources did you gain from that learning? (It is important to seek constructive learnings and resources here, rather than resentful ones. If you still have negative answers, keep asking: 'and what did all that give me' until you find at least two positive answers in a row.)

3. Begin to write "I'm looking for someone who..." with a list of qualities and behaviours that you would like in a partner, instead of those you might have experienced previously. For each item on the list, ask yourself: 'how would I know that I was experiencing that?'

Understanding the Past

In the past, we had no control over the relationship we had with our parents. As children we lack power and are in survival mode. In order to survive, we had to develop strategies to encourage our caregivers to keep us safe. We could not effectively challenge things we didn't like.

This is not about good or bad parenting; all children have to go through this and it is normal. Of course, it is worth noting here that some children grow up in environments that are very dangerous physically, psychologically or emotionally. Children in this environment may have to develop more extreme strategies to survive.

There is an interesting concept in psychology, known as 'family of origin'[18]. This is the idea that we develop a series of templates about people and not just those we will want to have romantic relationships with. In adulthood we unconsciously seek people to fit all the roles from our family of origin. Once identified we then attempt to re-enact the patterns we had with the original family members (totally out of conscious awareness). For example:

- Parenting our partner,
- 'Sibling rivalry' with partner (e.g. competitive for someone else's attention),
- Seeking approval, behaving childishly,
- Conspiring with our partner in being naughty or not taking responsibility,
- Sulking if our partner won't give us (or let us have) what we want.

The first step in being 'ready' for a relationship is 'self-awareness'. This involves identifying what we need to change in ourselves before seeking to change others. If we have an internal issue (i.e. an old hurt), no amount of seeking to change others will help this. Self-awareness helps us to recognise what we need to address within ourselves rather than focussing on others and trying to change them.

The place to start in increasing your self-awareness is to become aware of the patterns you may be recreating with your choice of partner. If you have had a number of partners, look for patterns and similarities. Even if you have only ever had one partner, you can look for the similarities with your parent figure.

You could also check who you have been attracted to, even if no relationship developed. If you have had a number of these, were they typically unavailable or not returning the attraction or did you simply admire from afar?

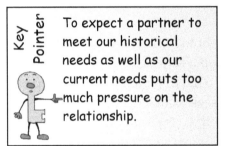

Key Pointer To expect a partner to meet our historical needs as well as our current needs puts too much pressure on the relationship.

As we develop self-awareness through seeking patterns, we then need to look for how we might address those patterns. We can do this by identifying what old/historical needs are not being met in our relationships and seek to meet those needs in other ways. To expect a partner to meet our historical needs as well as our current needs puts too much pressure on the relationship. Consider the following questions:

- What specifically have you wanted to change about your partner or partners? Write a list.
- For each thing you wanted to change, what is the need (or needs) within you that has not been met by your partner?
- How can you meet each of those needs for yourself?

Sometimes we need to go back to the relationship we have with our parents and look at how we are interacting with them as adults. We may still be playing out these old patterns even now. Do you ever experience a sense of regression when you spend time with your parents?

Addressing our original pattern is one of the most powerful ways to release yourself from repetitive and unsatisfying experiences. This is not about necessarily challenging our parents and confronting them, in many cases that would be inappropriate. It could even lead to your parents behaving in such a way that the pattern becomes more entrenched. Our parents are not the same people they were when we were children.

So, what do we need to do? There are many different approaches you can take. You could explore your family dynamics from a Transactional Analysis (TA) perspective. You could identify your life script and the patterns you are recreating. You could use TA approaches to change how you interact with others[19].

Alternatively, you could take an NLP or hypnosis/hypnotherapy approach. There are many interventions within NLP that are specifically designed to help you change limiting beliefs, automatic emotional responses and to update your map of the world[20].

Handling the Past

Some people have less than ideal formative/early years with unmet needs, traumas and poor role models. Part of the solution in this case might include effective therapy and/or transformational workshops. However, even when faced with painful pasts, some people still grow up healthy whilst some transform old hurts by making a decision that they will not let the past run them anymore.

Other people seem to have had 'idyllic' childhoods and yet they still seem rather unbalanced. Indeed, some may have particular family patterns where they absolutely idolise one of their parents. Even as adults, they don't appear to have psychologically grown up beyond the apron strings or hero worship. Of course, this scenario can be just as damaging to a grown-up relationship as resentment and hurt (especially if partners are being compared unfavourably to parents… for example mama's cooking or daddy's fixing things!)

It is important to understand the 'positive intentions' of hanging on to old stuff. What does it give a person to stay stuck in old ways and patterns? Might it give them protection, a story/talking point, an identity? If you realise that you have 'stuff' from the past that you have yet to let go of, ask yourself this question: What do you get by hanging on to that 'stuff'? What does that give you? Often, the first response is 'nothing'. Take a deep breath and ask yourself again. Common reasons for hanging on include: protection and safety, comfort, avoidance of pain etc.

As you develop and grow into the confident, brilliant, balanced and constructive you, remember that no-one is totally perfect or 'enlightened'. We are all somewhat neurotic and pathological! As long as your 'old stuff' doesn't hurt you or your partner, accept and acknowledge your 'foibles'. If your neurosis is not limiting or hurtful, then it may simply be termed a 'quirk' or 'eccentricity' or 'what makes you different'.

It may not surprise you to realise that in order to have better relationships we need to start by looking at ourselves. As we move toward self-actualisation we will naturally enjoy more fulfilling relationships!

Part Two: Creating the perfect dance partner

If birds do it and bees do it, why is it sometimes so challenging for people to do it? We are, of course, talking about finding a relationship and falling in love. Obviously, it helps if you can find someone to fall in love with who also falls in love with you. However, for those who are single but wish to be otherwise engaged, are you *really* ready for a new relationship? Is there a 'relationship shaped space' in your life?

So, when *you* are ready, what can *you* do to find your potential partner? How can *you* create the opportunities to meet the right kind of person for you?

a) <u>Creating your Partner</u>

If you have answered the questions above, you have already begun the next phase and if you have not then you are about to begin (unless you are reading this section simply from a point of curiosity!) It is time to get outcome focused and create your new partner.

Take an hour or so to write what you want in a partner. We will call this a 'template'. Write everything you can think of, from their physical appearance to their behaviours, values, goals and interests. Write everything in terms of what you want, rather than what you do not want (e.g. rather than 'I don't want someone who is already in a relationship', write something like 'I want someone who is single and available to me'.) Include as much detail as you can...do they want kids or not want kids? Do they want to travel or not travel?

Now have a look at what you have written and run it through some checks. Use these checks to make sure your template is as healthy as possible and will give you what you really want:

1) Check your 'template' for ambiguity (i.e. things that could be interpreted in other ways). One of our clients did this exercise and realised that much of what he had written (e.g. blond hair, brown eyes, loyal and affectionate) could also describe a golden retriever!

2) Check your template for 'positive intentions'. As you look through it, continually ask yourself: 'and what would that give me?' or 'what would I gain by having that?' The idea here is to understand *why* you want what you want and perhaps challenge how healthy some of the things might be. For example: "I want my partner to make me the centre of their world and to love only me" – is this reasonable? Can they not have friends or family?

3) Connected to the 'positive intentions' is to check for 'unintended consequences'. Ask: 'If I had someone with that quality/characteristic, might there be any downsides?' For

example: "I want someone who would dote on me and wants to be with me all the time". Could this have a dark side if it went too far? A partner who wants to know where you are at all times and won't even let you close the lavatory door!

4) Check that your template is truly balanced and constructive; otherwise, you are inviting 'drama' (the kind of thing people complain to others about, get upset about and at extreme, end up on some daytime television programme about!) For example, some people say they want passion in a relationship because a 'peaceful' relationship would be boring. How much 'drama' do you *really* want in your relationship? Is it possible to experience excitement and passion without it being unbalanced, destructive and/or painful? How might you have balanced-constructive engagement and excitement?

When you have completed the template (and checked it for ambiguity and 'unintended consequences'), put it to one side for at least 24 hours. When you return to the template, read it through and then ask yourself: 'Am I the sort of person that the person I'm creating would want to be with?' This is not designed to be a 'beat myself up' exercise, so if that begins to happen...stop doing that and read the next section!

b) Creating the Ready You

What, if anything, do you need to do so that you are ready to have a relationship with the person you are looking for? Do you have space (psychological, time, energy) for someone else in your life? What personal development have you done since your last relationship? How have you grown and in what areas? Looking at the kind of person you want in your life, how would you fit with that template you have created? How do you treat others...what feedback have you had in the past?

As you read the chapters in this book, consider these questions:

- In what ways would you and a new partner be *complimentary*?
- How could you strive to be *interdependent* with them?
- How might you identify that you are becoming an advancing or retreating energy and how might you return to a balance point?
- When faced with difference, how might you behave? How would you like to behave?

c) Creating the Opportunities

Some people seem to believe that finding a good relationship is simply a matter of luck. Richard Wiseman[20] has studied the area of luck extensively and has concluded that those who are deemed 'lucky' appear to be more aware of their environment than those who are labelled 'unlucky'.

Indeed, way back in time, a first century Roman philosopher called Seneca suggested that luck is what happens when preparation meets opportunity. If luck is at the crossroads of preparation and opportunity, this chapter so far has primarily been about personal preparation. So, to help you find the crossroads, here are some strategies that people have for creating relationship *opportunities*:

- Go to what Phil McGraw[22] calls: 'target rich environments'. Where would the kind of person you'd like to meet hang out? Join clubs and societies. Go to meetings, courses and events. Talk to interesting people. If, for example, you are interested in wildlife and would like to meet a partner who shared this interest, volunteer for a wildlife charity.
- Go to places that are traditionally likely to have more people of the gender you are looking for. As a man looking for a woman, if you like dancing, go to dance classes. As a woman looking for a man, join a golf club!
- Wherever you are... whether at a party, at work or at some other event, use your senses and be aware of your

environment. Keep your eyes open. Notice the other people who are around you. Listen. Some people seem to completely miss that someone else is showing an interest or asking them on a date! Follow your heart. You do not have to date everyone who shows interest. Be selective and yet open to possibilities. Be prepared to take a risk and make the first move. Recognise that 'no' is not a rejection of *you* but simply a response to your invitation.

Seek those who treat you how you want to be treated. Challenge or let go of those who treat you less than well. If something doesn't feel right at the start, take time to reflect rather than ignore it. The way someone treats you at the start of the relationship (particularly destructive behaviour) is indicative of how that person will behave in the future. Can you *really* live with that behaviour ongoing?

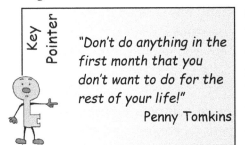

Key Pointer

"Don't do anything in the first month that you don't want to do for the rest of your life!"

Penny Tomkins

Any unusual traits a new partner might have (e.g. highly extrovert after a few drinks) may seem endearing or tolerable at the start...but how will that work for you in five years' time?

The final words on creating your 'desired outcome' partner are, of course: "If what you are doing isn't working, do something different." Learn from what seems to work and what does not. Get creative. Enjoy the process of meeting new people. Be ready to fall in love all over again!

A final note

We have the ability to change our beliefs, patterns and emotional responses. Often, we need the help and support of others, however ultimately, we make these changes for ourselves. One of the presuppositions[23] (empowering beliefs) of neuro-linguistic programming is:

"We have all the resources we need within us!"

We believe this is true! We have the ability to change and this ability is within each and every one of us. What needs to be added is the fact that as human beings we are social animals. We are meant to have relationships, not just romantic but also friendships and family. By freeing ourselves from unhealthy patterns we are allowing ourselves the opportunity to engage in healthy relationships with *all* the people we care about.

Chapter 6

The Complementary Relationship

Understanding and Creating Compatibility

"At last I met a pretty girl, she laughed and talked with me.
We both walked out of the kitchen and danced in a new way."

Jona Lewie *"Kitchen at Parties"*

In This Chapter...

In this chapter, we will be introducing you to the idea of a 'complementary' relationship where both partners can exist in harmony with one another, utilising their differences and their strengths.

We will be exploring the following questions:

- What is a complementary relationship?
- How can you use the Five Relationship Graces to form agreements together?
- What are the 'components of compatibility'?
- How can you utilise your differences and make complementary decisions?

What is a Complementary Relationship?

A complementary relationship is the very essence of being **balanced-constructive**. A complementary couple dance in harmony with one another, they are in step and synchronised. They work well with one another, they match each other and have an apparently effortless rapport.

A complementary couple are different to one another and yet they utilise their differences, staying on the same side as they communicate and innovate, creating wonderful dynamics and harmonics together. They won't always agree but how they disagree is balanced and constructive.

Contracting and the Five Relationship Graces

'Contracting' is the process of establishing boundaries and forging agreements. It does not necessarily entail a formal, written contract. Indeed, our use of it here is in the context of relationships and might be termed more correctly: 'psychological contracting'.

As we go through this chapter, particularly if you are following the activities with your partner, it is important to hold the Five Relationship Graces in mind and heart as you share your thoughts and feelings. The agreements will allow you to be vulnerable and honest with one another. Here is a reminder:

1. **Care** *(ongoing maintenance)*
    We will place purposeful attention and effort into caring for and developing our relationship. We will continue to make the maintenance of our relationship a high priority, no matter what else happens in life.

2. **Kindness** *(open communication)*
    We will speak our truth with kindness and listen to one another even when the topic is less than easy. We will always be willing to communicate with one another.

3. **Respect** *(constructive action)*
    We will act constructively towards one another, particularly
    when it comes to our differences. We will speak respectfully
    about one another when we are with others.

4. **Compassion** *(balanced expectations)*
    We will act to meet each other's needs as well as our own and
    we will endeavour to be balanced in our expectations of one
    another.

5. **Dignity** *(joint ownership)*
    Without blame, we will take ownership of our own feelings,
    thoughts and actions. We will hold ourselves to account in
    staying with these agreements.

As part of the complementary contracting process in this chapter, we
would recommend that you begin with owning the five agreements,
saying them to one another from the first person, "I".

> I will place purposeful attention and effort into caring for and
> developing our relationship. I will continue to make the
> maintenance of our relationship a high priority, no matter
> what else happens in life.

> I will always be willing to communicate with you. I will speak
> my truth with kindness and listen to you even when the topic
> is less than easy.

> I will act constructively towards you, particularly when it
> comes to our differences. I will speak respectfully about you
> when I am with others.

> I will act to meet your needs as well as my own and I will
> endeavour to be balanced in my expectations of you.

> Without blame, I will take ownership of my own feelings, thoughts and actions. I will hold myself to account in staying with these agreements.

How does it feel to say these words and to hear them from your partner? Hear the words and allow yourself to trust the process.

Contracting through the 'Components of Compatibility'

When two people come together in relationship, each brings their own unique personality (sense of identity, beliefs, values, expectations, strengths and 'development areas'). The question then becomes: "How compatible are we?"

There is a model which can be used as a tool for contracting: establishing and communicating the similarities, differences and complements between you and your partner. By highlighting the challenges and resources between you, this will give you an opportunity to proactively prevent issues rather than having to reactively handle irreconcilable problems later. The model was created by Robert Dilts[24] and is known as the 'neurological levels'. In the context of this book, we are using the 'levels' as a framework of components. This will provide some key categories for questions to ask one another.

When you and your partner are agreeable (and are in the right place and mood to discuss important matters), take some time together to consider some of the following questions. If you get stuck or uncover a significant difference, have a look at Chapter 8 ("Practical Steps to Handling Differences"):

1) Environment
   - Where do you want to go in life?
   - What do you want to do in life?
   - What environment do you want to live in?

- What would be the ideal type of house/home/accommodation for you?
- How do you like your environment? E.g. open space, cluttered, colourful, minimalist…?

2) Behaviour

When it is just the two of you alone or when you are in the company of others:

- How do you wish to be treated?
- What do you especially like?
- What do you especially dislike?
- What would be your deal-breakers?

3) Capability

- What strengths do you bring to the relationship?
- What are you good at and what do you enjoy?
- What do you want to achieve in your life?
- What do you want to develop and get better at?
- What do you want to learn in life?

4) Beliefs and Values

- What are some of your beliefs around politics, religion, money etc.? Where do you stand?
- What is true for you about relationships?
- What would be an ideal relationship?
- What is important to you about relationships?
- What is important to you about: e.g. children, extended family, friends, work, leisure time, holidays, sex, money?

5) Identity

- How much personal space and time do you like?
- Who are you when you are 'being yourself'?
- What legacy do you want to leave personally?

6) Spirit
- As a couple and individually, what do you wish to contribute to your community?
- How do you want to make a positive difference in the world?
- What are your joint life goals? What do you want to achieve together?

These questions are not designed to create an 'annual appraisal' of one another, they are meant to open up discussion, to express your values and goals, and to learn more about your partner's values and goals. Some may be similar and some may be different.

Of course, these questions can be addressed at any stage of life and relationship. We cannot help but change and refine and develop. If the questions highlight a difference we are usually better off discussing our expectations with a view to finding an encompassing 'win/win' solution that we can both be happy with. A relationship where either partner feels stuck or compromised is likely to be a relationship with resentment. We know of couples who have discovered after two or three years of marriage that one of them wanted children and the other one didn't. Perhaps this would have been useful information earlier in the relationship.

Contracting the 'Tough Stuff': Deal-breakers

For couples to thrive (as opposed to simply survive), it is helpful if they have an understanding of what makes the other tick. Further still, it will be important that they agree what works for them in the relationship… what is okay and what is not okay? Although we might like to think of our relationship as limitless, there will still be boundaries. When boundaries are crossed, Phil McGraw[25] calls these situations: 'deal-breakers'. For many couples, infidelity would be an example of a boundary crossed, and hence a deal-breaker.

In a culture where forty to fifty percent of marriages end in separation (often due to 'irreconcilable differences'), would it not be preferable to be honest and up-front as to what works and what doesn't? Why wait until your partner crosses an ill-defined boundary to speak up about what you want and don't want in your relationship?

What would you regard as your 'deal-breakers'? What behaviours might your partner do that would be absolutely unacceptable to you? When you and your partner are ready, take some time so that you can both share what would cross your boundaries. Remember to stay with the Five Relationship Graces as you talk and listen.

Creating Complementary Differences

A 'model' relationship tends to work on the basis of both parties communicating their needs and expectations. This is done with the intention of finding solutions that will encompass the needs and expectations of both sides. This way, neither side feels they have lost out or been compromised in some way.

Successful couples listen to one another with a desire to resolve differences and create agreements. Put simply, where there is a difference, they seek the common ground. Where there is agreement, they build.

Even where there is a difference in goals or interests, how might you both support one another in pursuing these things without them becoming detrimental to your relationship? This may be an opportunity to talk about boundaries. How far are you prepared to go to support your partner and what would cross the line? For example, how much time apart pursuing activities can you both happily accept (and how much time would you prefer to spend together)? How much money might each of you reasonably spend on your goals and interests?

As well as perhaps having individual pursuits, what interests and goals do you share? What do you both enjoy doing? Where can you spend time together in joint pursuits?

In Chapter 8 we will explore more about difference and how successful couples handle difference before it becomes conflict.

Complementary Decision Making

In the past, we have seen issues in some relationships where decision making becomes unbalanced. One partner becomes 'responsible' for how things are done and the other partner gives up responsibility. Of course, this means if things go wrong, they get to blame each other! One gets blamed for making the wrong decision and the other gets blamed for not taking responsibility and getting involved. One partner might give up responsibility in the hope of an 'easier life'. However, in our experience, making your partner responsible for decision making rarely leads to an easier life!

Complementary decision making requires both partners to take responsibility for expressing their opinion, seeking agreement, making the decision and owning the outcome and consequences. There is no need or desire here for the blame game! If a couple does choose to delegate out some of the decision making, it is essential that there is balance (so one person is not making more decisions than the other) and an acceptance that whatever one decides, the other will back that decision.

So, consider for a moment how you make decisions as a couple, for example:

- *About money?* Some couples have a totally transparent approach to money, where earnings and expenditure are visible to both partners; they might have a joint account where all income goes into a single pot. Some prefer to keep their accounts separate and personal. Others may fit somewhere in between, perhaps with a joint account and then separate accounts too. What if one partner earns more than the other: do they get more financial or spending 'rights'? Or does the couple maintain equality no matter who earns what?

- *About children?* The first decision is "do we have children?" and then there are hundreds of questions to address after that! Children are smart and if they see a loophole or a chink in the armour of parent solidarity, they will often exploit it.

A Case In Point

We thought long and hard about having children. Neither of us was particularly driven to have them and there was no 'biological imperative'. In our 'final decision' conversation, we were both pretty clear that the answer was 'no'. However, when I considered how I felt I realised it was a 97% "no". When I checked with Joe, he was clear that his "no" was 100%. We spent some time discussing this and I realised that I needed to know that if I really wanted to have children that Joe would be open to making that choice.

I was pretty clear about my answer but I did not want to look back on this decision in twenty-year's time with any feelings of regret, or worse resentment. Joe realised how important this was to me and took some time to reflect and was able to give me that choice. Although he didn't want children he was prepared to change his position if it was that important to me.

Paradoxically this allowed me to confirm my decision, I did not want to have children. Now almost twenty years on from that discussion we are both happy with that decision and clear that we both had the freedom to make a choice independently of each other.

Melody

- *About family?* Later in a relationship, there can sometimes be tough choices to make about the welfare of elderly parents. Before that point however, there may be decisions to make about how to handle interference. We have met lots of couples where there is a tension resulting from intrusive or manipulative extended-family members (e.g. parents and siblings). The problem is often with one of the couple not wanting to 'take sides'. Their partner therefore doesn't feel supported and the tension remains. So, whose side are you on? This doesn't mean that you always side with your partner, especially if they don't want to associate with your family at all! You both need to get clear about your boundaries and needs and then discuss these alone as a couple.

- *About pets?* How often have you heard about one partner surprising the other with a pet? Who takes care of that animal? Do they do it joyfully or grudgingly? If pets are bought for children, again, who will be looking after the pets (and who will look after the pets when the children leave home)?

- *About holidays?* What kind of holidays do you both like? Do you go on holiday to relax, explore, adventure, play, shop, be entertained, eat, drink and be merry? Are you both sun worshippers? Where have you been and where do you want to visit? What have been your favourite outings in the past?

- *About recreation?* What kind of things do you both like doing in your spare time? Are they the same or at least the same type of things (e.g. sport, shopping, collecting)?

- *About traditions?* Some people have traditions that they like to fulfil, perhaps around seasonal festivals (e.g. Christmas) and annual events (e.g. Bonfire night). Some of these traditions may be quite nostalgic and important to the individual. What traditions do you each bring to the relationship? How might you involve each other so they become 'our' tradition?

Of course, there are lots of contexts in which you will make decisions and things that you will need to make decisions about. The important question is HOW you make decisions. What process do you go through (that you can utilise no matter WHAT you are deciding)?

By having a process, you will be better able to handle surprise situations. In addition, you can make hypothetical or retrospective decisions... "If that happens (again) then we will..."

What process might you use?

Here are some steps to consider in making decisions together.

1) Acknowledge/communicate that a decision needs to be made?
2) Agree that a decision is required and by when.
3) Share opinions, recognising that initially, they are just ideas. Stay open to ideas and explore rather than shut down (e.g. "tell me more about that" or "what would we get by doing that?")
4) If necessary, talk about the pros and cons of ideas.
5) Select the best idea (or be open to a new best idea emerging – perhaps one that combines your ideas in some way, giving you the best of both worlds). For more details on this, see the next chapter.
6) Take action and own the consequences!

Complementary Compliments

As we shall see in the next chapter, it seems that successful couples openly compliment one another (as well as complement one another). They tend to focus on what they like their partner doing rather than criticising what they don't like. That doesn't mean that they remain silent about things that are bothering them, but when they do, they do it in a loving manner.

> **A Case In Point**
>
> Years ago, I asked Joe if he would print off some compliment slips for me. What he brought me was a rather nice surprise! As well as the requested business compliment slips, he also gave me a pile of paper slips with lots of different compliments on them. Things like "You are beautiful" and "I'm glad I met you". I still have them to this day!
>
> Melody

The Complementary Couple

When two people model the spirit of a complementary relationship they celebrate and integrate difference. They admire and enjoy their constructive differences (i.e. those that support and do not interfere with the relationship) and they seek to find mutually agreeable solutions when faced with conflicting differences (i.e. those that might otherwise polarise and split the relationship).

Whatever life throws at the 'complementary couple', they start from the basis that *they are on the same side*. They work together as a partnership, as a team. They understand and respect each other's expectations and boundaries. They seek the common ground and they build.

Chapter 7

Communicating Relationships

*"Without communication, the relationship sinks
beneath the waters of confusion."*

Joe

In This Chapter...

This chapter will explore how to find your balance point when communicating with your partner (e.g. *how* do you communicate what you need and what is important to you?)

It will help you (and your partner) reflect on your own styles and hence, how you might communicate with one another more healthily and in a more balanced-constructive manner.

We will be exploring the following questions:

- How can you express your ideas and opinions with kindness?
- What is balanced-constructive communication?
- How might you handle unbalanced or destructive reactions?
- What are some healthy ways of asking for what you want?
- How do you give and receive feedback effectively?
- What are some effective ways of making and taking apologies?

The challenge in any relationship is to find ways of communicating fairly, kindly and cleanly particularly when talking about 'difficult' and/or 'emotive' things. In chapter 2, we used a metaphor of the 'tunnel' between partners. In this chapter, we are looking at how we can prevent the tunnel becoming foggy, particularly when it comes to talking about feelings, needs and values.

Expressing your truth with kindness

The second of our Five Relationship Graces is about communication; it includes the phrase: "speaking our truth with kindness". We find communication to be the lynch-pin of our relationship and have seen what happens when, in the past, we might have forgotten this. Communication is a big, broad concept however. It is important, of course, to talk with your partner and it is equally important as to *how* you do this. We sometimes encounter couples who are not good at taking time to talk with one another; and we encounter even more who do not communicate well at all.

'Speaking your truth with kindness' means being prepared to state what you need, how you feel and/or what is important to you, whilst at the same time doing it in such a way that it is presented with respect, love, fairness, and reasonableness. We extend this 'mantra' out to any interaction we have with others, even 'complaining' in a restaurant.

The first step in 'expressing your truth' is (rather obviously) knowing what your truth *is* in a given situation. Here are some questions that may help:

- How exactly am I feeling (e.g. a specific emotion, a mix of emotions, confused, hurt, proud, delighted)?
- What specifically do I want/need here? (And what would I get by having that?)
- What is *really* important to me here?
- *What is my truth here and now?*

Part of knowing your truth is to *own* it. Be responsible for your own feelings, wants and needs. Your truth is *your* truth and not necessarily true for others. If you feel like someone is not listening to you, you might say: "I feel like you are not listening to me" rather than "you are not listening to me" (which is also known a 'mind-read' because we don't really know if someone is listening or not).

And what about the 'with kindness' part? Once you know your own truth in a situation (i.e. how you feel, what you need), take a mental trip to the other person's world. Be prepared for the fact that they may have a different truth. Be prepared to share, listen and discuss rather than demand. Allow yourself to communicate without blame or accusation; understand that there *is* another side. Stay empathetic to them as well as expressing your side.

Consider these questions:

- How might what I am saying be interpreted?
- How might they be feeling?
- What might they want/need here? (And what would they get by having that?)
- What could be important to them here?
- *How might I express myself with them, here and now?*

The reason the questions about others are in the form of 'might' and 'could' is that we will never truly *know* until we ask them. To assume we know what someone else is thinking/feeling is not a helpful place for true communication because we are still wrapped up in *our own* world. We can, however, start with an educated guess and work from there… being open to the possibility of being incorrect!

When we are truly *expressing ourselves with kindness*, we are communicating from **balanced-constructive**.

Balanced-Constructive Communication

In order to understand what balanced-constructive communication would look like (i.e. clean/healthy), let us also look at the alternative (i.e. unclean/unhealthy).

1) Unbalanced
   - Retreating: minimal communication (both in frequency and content), not saying enough to be clear/understood, hiding.
   - Advancing: too much communication (important points are diluted by other content), exaggerated (things blown out of proportion).

2) Destructive
   - Avoidance: Changing subject, (I don't want to talk about it), walking away.
   - Apprehension: Walls are up, guarded, hedging around a topic.
   - Antagonism: Critical, accusatory, blame, attacking or counter-attacking, over generalised language (e.g. you never, you always, you should)
   - Aversion: Insulting, potentially abusive, threatening, bullying, 'disowned' (focus on 'you') language (e.g. *you* make me, the problem with *you* is, *your* problem is)

3) Balanced Constructive
   - Honest (with self as well as with partner),
   - Clear
   - Owned
   - Considered (responsive rather than reactive),
   - Positively stated towards what you want; outcome oriented (it goes somewhere)
   - Purposeful (there is a point to it and a reason behind it).

- Mindful of and empathetic to the other person.
- Based in the 'here and now' rather than representing history.

A Case In Point

In the early days of our relationship, when we were going out we would agree what time we needed to be at the venue. However, we seemed to have a different perception of how long the journey would take. I like to get there on time and Melody prefers to be early. This meant she tended to be ready before me... and she would be getting impatient as she stood by the front door with her coat on! By the time we got into the car there was a hint of tension... not the greatest start to going out somewhere!

Since something wasn't working we changed our 'going out strategy'. We now ask: "What time do we need to be there?" *and then* "so what time do we want to leave the house?" This allows us to discuss our predicted journey time and agree something that is within our control (i.e. leaving time). This rally works for us and over time, the level of discussion needed has diminished and is no longer an issue.

If one of us is not ready to leave on time, we might say that the agreement has been broken and I guess we could get annoyed with that if we chose to! The reality is, we get there when we get there... and usually we get there on time.

Joe

Communicating with Expression and Empathy

To *speak your truth with kindness* is an **assertive** form of communication: being prepared to express yourself whilst having empathy for the other person's perspective. The alternatives are:

- If someone has *expression without empathy*, they are likely to come across as **aggressive** (i.e. expressing their opinions, views, rights, feelings, needs, wants, values and beliefs *without caring* about the other person's opinions, views, rights, feelings, needs, wants, values and beliefs).
- If someone has *empathy without expression*, they are likely to come across as **passive** (i.e. accepting the other person's opinions, views, rights, feelings, needs, wants, values and beliefs *at the expense of their own*).
- If someone has *neither expression nor empathy*, they are likely to come across as **indirect** and manipulative (i.e. being unclear about their own opinions, views, rights, feelings, needs, wants, values and beliefs whilst also not caring for the other person's).

To behave and communicate **assertively** is a balanced combination of expression *and* empathy (i.e. to care for yourself *and* your partner). Other examples of assertive communication might be:

- *Seeking win/win*: finding approaches and solutions that work for both of you.
- *Exploration*: Asking questions about and listening to your partner's needs.
- *Openness*: Being open about what you want and why.
- *Boundaries*: Being clear about what you don't want (or what is 'off the table').

Handling Reactions

What if you communicate with your partner and it seems to go wrong? What if you are misunderstood despite your best intentions and endeavours? What if they get defensive or aggressive?

First things first, we have found it essential for couples to establish a communication 'culture' where it is okay for a partner to say something that may be difficult to talk about. We both need to be able to trust our partner (and ourselves) that we can be safe to express needs and feelings, to be vulnerable and open our hearts. This is something that couples need to agree as a kind of 'ground-rule' at some point in the relationship. The easiest time, of course, tends to be at the beginning – but we have found that it is never too late for a couple to sit down and agree how they wish to be treated. A good place to start would be the Five Relationship Graces (outlined in the Introduction).

This agreement sits within the 'contracting' segment in the last chapter, where you establish your boundaries and preferences. As an example, in terms of communication, some of our own 'unwritten' rules are:

- The communicator takes responsibility for *when* and *how* they choose to communicate, as well as *what*.
- Create an appropriate time and space for a conversation (i.e. not when we are dashing around or engrossed in something like a favourite TV show). We respect each other's time and space. We might say something along the lines of: "When you have finished doing that, there's something I'd like to talk with you about."
- Respect each other. There is no need for blame or accusation. Even if one of us is doing something the other doesn't like, it is still done from the perspective of: "I find that annoying!" or "I don't really like it when you…" rather than "you are annoying!"
- Clean, owned expressions of our own feelings/needs. Establish how we feel about the situation and then what we would prefer to have happen. Also, understand if this is 'old stuff' being retriggered (which may have nothing to do with our partner really).
- When looking for a solution or decision, we always seek a way forward that we are both happy with. (This is discussed further in the next chapter.)

- Voice tonality is kind and loving wherever possible rather than harsh and/or angry.
- If our words or delivery is not really how we meant to deliver it (we are human – we do make mistakes and we do get annoyed from time to time), then we will apologise!
- We sometimes ask one another how we would like to be communicated with.

A Case In Point

If 'A' is communicating with 'B', who is responsible for making sure that 'B' gets the message?
- Is it 'A' the communicator?
- Is it 'B' the listener?
- Is it both?

Here's our take on it... whichever we happen to be, 'A' or 'B', we will take 100% responsibility to make sure the communication has taken place. That way, there is no blame (e.g. "you didn't explain properly"/ "you didn't listen"), there is simply 100% ownership.

It is important to remember that you can take responsibility to communicate as clearly and cleanly as possible but you can't control how your partner might react at a given moment in time. If the response you get is not constructive, go back to the ideas discussed in Chapter 4 on **remaining balanced and constructive**. After you have resolved a specific conversation, check with yourself that you were clean, clear and healthy in your delivery – was there anything you did or said that might have provoked your partner? If necessary, ask them how they would have preferred to have had that discussion.

It may be worth including 'tonality' in your assessment (i.e. *how* the words were spoken). Balanced words can become irrelevant and unheard if delivered in a sarcastic or parental tone of voice.

Asking for what we want

There will be times in relationship when our partner does something we like or does something we don't like. We then have a decision whether to say something about it or not. If we like something they do, it seems a shame not to at least thank them! If they are doing something we dislike, is it something we can tolerate/accept or will it cause greater irritation and fester over time?

This segment of the book addresses situations where:

- we want to give our partner 'feedback',
- there is something we need them to do,
- there is something they are doing that we would like them to do differently,
- they are doing something we like and we'd like them to do it more often,
- we simply want to appreciate our partner for something.

Many people find it less than easy to ask for what they want. Instead, they either 'put up' with things perhaps resentfully, or they may resort to indirect methods of communication. If one partner says "I'm a bit cold", what does that actually mean? Are they expecting their partner to 'mind-read' them in some way? This may seem a minor issue but it can be indicative of a style of communication that can cause friction and tensions. Consider some possible interpretations and responses to "I'm a bit cold":

Interpretation	Response
It is a simple statement of fact…	"Oh dear."
They are seeking sympathy/ attention…	"Oh, you poor thing."
They are seeking empathy/ understanding/ validation…	"Yes, me too. It is cold."
It is a problem to solve…	"I'll put the heating on."

These are some relatively constructive responses! The partner (if being destructive) might say: "Stop whining" or "Put a jumper on then".

If your partner is prone to indirect communication, a useful response might be: "What do you need?" This invites them to be clear with you as to what they require, for example: empathy, a cuddle, for you to pass their jumper to them, for you to light the fire or put the heating on…

Healthy and unhealthy approaches

When it comes to asking for what you want from your partner, we could say that there are *healthy* and *unhealthy* approaches. Let us start with some unhealthy ones:

a) Unbalanced – Advancing
   If you are generally an advancing energy, beware of trying to change your partner beyond all recognition! It is rather sad when two people fall in love, only to have one partner try to change the other, then later say: "You're not the person I fell in love with!" Before 'giving feedback', an advancing energy may need to ask themselves: "Is it about them or really about me? Is it impacting elsewhere within our relationship or outside? Did I once find this endearing? What do I need to do to accept what they are doing?"

b) Unbalanced – Retreating
   If you are generally the retreating/withdrawing energy, don't blame your partner for not giving you what you want if you don't ask them! It is important for a withdrawing energy to give feedback if something is wrong. Without this communication, the other person may not be aware that you are unhappy. A retreating energy may need to ask themselves: "What is not working here? How do I feel and

about what specifically? What do I need to do differently and what could my partner do differently? What do I need from them?"

c) Destructive

If you have a tendency to criticise your partner, put them down, deride them or become sarcastic to them, be aware of the impact this may be having on the relationship. Even if you feel irritated by your partner, resorting to destructive behaviours can only erode the bond you have between you. It is sad when one or both partners feel they must put their partner down in some way to feel better about themselves (which, ironically, doesn't actually work). Someone with a typically destructive energy needs to address their own self esteem (see Chapter 5). If they want their partner to change in some way, they may need to ask themselves: "What am I not happy about? What might I be doing to perpetuate this situation? Is it really them that needs to change? What do I need from my partner instead of what they are currently doing? How can I be supportive to them?"

A *healthy* approach would be **balanced-constructive**. Here, there is a desire to be happy whilst helping to maintain the happiness of your partner. Here are some questions you might ask yourself:

- What do I want to achieve by giving them feedback here?
- If I'm not happy about something, what specifically do I feel? What do I want from them? What do *I* need to do to help that happen?
- If I am happy about something, what exactly is my partner doing (or what have they done) and what is it I like about it?

If you would like a model or structure for saying what you need to say, here are some ideas. Remember, they are just ideas and not a script to read out!

- Steps to 'asking for change': Tell them what you are experiencing currently and how you feel about that. Empathise with them if possible (e.g. "I understand that you were letting off steam"). Say what you would like from them (e.g. "instead of shouting at me, talk to me – tell me what's going on"). When it comes to simple things, for example a favour, we sometimes use a simpler: "can you do something for me…" or "can you do me a favour…" or "I'd really appreciate it if you…"
- Steps to 'appreciating' your partner (i.e. when you like what your partner is doing or has done): Tell them what they have done, why you like it and thank them (for example: "I don't know if you are aware of this, but when you say I look handsome, I really like that. I feel a greater sense of confidence. Thank you.")

What if our partner reacts badly to the feedback?

Of course, the fear of giving feedback is usually driven by the thought that it might make things worse (e.g. start an argument). Here are some ideas for preventing and handling a negative reaction to feedback:

- Check the content: is the feedback useful for them or it is more for you? Will it genuinely benefit them in some way or are you trying to stop them doing something that bugs you?
- Check the delivery: how did you deliver the feedback? Could your delivery have been misunderstood? If the feedback had been delivered to you in that way, how would you have felt? What do you know about your partner and your differences… how do *they* like to receive feedback?
- Check the context (i.e. the where and the when): was it really the best time and place?
- In terms of handling the reaction itself (e.g. angry, counterattack), have a look the section on 'Remaining Balanced Constructive' in Chapter 4.

- Check the reaction/response: how well did they take the feedback?

Handling feedback from your partner

Why do we sometimes struggle to hear or take feedback? For many, even being given constructive praise or appreciation can cause discomfort and/or a defensive reaction e.g.: "This old thing?" or "what are *they* after?"

When our partner asks us to do something differently, what makes us react internally? A classic response to being given feedback or being asked to change is a feeling of defensiveness. Even if it is a simple thing, we might behave as if our very identity is being threatened! Of course, if we find ourselves reacting *that* strongly to a simple request, it would tend to indicate a retriggering of 'old stuff'.

When someone asks us to change (or change the way we do something), it can generate all sorts of possible internal reactions, e.g. "I'm not good enough", "they don't love me anymore", "how dare they, it's not as if they're perfect" or "seriously??"

Consider how you tend to react, both to praise/appreciation and to a request for change. Can you stay balanced-constructive?

Understanding the unbalanced reaction to feedback

In the field of neuro-linguistic programming there is a model called 'metaprograms'[26] which are underlying unconscious filters through which we experience life in order to make decisions, sort information, respond and communicate. One meta-program in particular is a description of how we are 'referenced' (externally, internally or somewhere in between).

A person is **internally referenced** if they rely on their own evaluation of their behaviour and context. They are *completely* internally referenced in that context if they totally disregard, ignore or even delete evaluations from other people. For the person who is more **externally referenced**, they will be keen to receive feedback from others, to know the consensus view and the norms.

If we combine this concept with the advancing and retreating energies, these would give us some of the potential reactions and defences to feedback. Remember that the table below shows the unbalanced responses of extremes. We will explore the balanced response on the next page.

	Internally Referenced		
Advancing	May ask for feedback and say they are open to it but may then disregard it or justify/ explain it away. They know best and will fight to be right.	Will not ask for (or welcome) feedback. May seem to ignore what is said, perhaps with minimal response. They may reflect but more on their own thoughts.	**Retreating**
	Will seek feedback from others (perhaps excessively), seeking validation from others. May feel that others must be right.	Will not necessarily seek feedback but will ruminate over what has been said to them, playing comments over in their mind.	
	Externally Referenced		

As a further note about **internally referenced** folk, imagine a situation where one person in the relationship is **internally referenced** in regard to their behaviour towards their partner. They are likely to ignore, disregard or explain away their partner's opinions and expressions of unhappiness. If this goes on for any length of time the relationship may ultimately break up. For the

internally referenced person, there may be the experience of one relationship after another breaking up for "no apparent reason". If you recognise that you are unable to sustain a relationship and that you regularly take a position of being right, perhaps you might want to consider examining how you process feedback from others. You may not want to do this of course, but only you can decide whether your happiness is important enough for you to consider some alternatives. These are just some suggestions and only you will know if they are valid for your experience and life.

A balanced-constructive response

The balance in terms of 'internally/externally referenced' will be somewhere in the middle, with a mixture of both. This allows us to hear someone else's feedback (and perhaps gather evidence from other people) as well as using our own intuition and judgement. Simply put, feedback is data. It is important to gather data and then make an informed decision as to what we want to do with it.

Perhaps one of the easiest ways to stay 'healthy' is to ask your partner for more information (which may be the opposite to what we feel inside!) Ask questions like:

- Can you tell me more about what you're saying?
- When do I do that?
- What is it specifically that you don't like?
- What do you need from me in that situation?

Other things you might do:

- Ask for feedback from someone else who knows you well enough to be straight with you. (They may be reluctant to do so of course if in the past you have had a tendency to ignore feedback!)

- Write down all the feedback without comment. Thank the person and then quietly reflect on what you have written down. You might want to make a note of your internal response to the feedback as well.
- Ask yourself: "Have I received this feedback before?" If the answer is "yes", it might be worth considering how often and from whom? A general rule of thumb we follow is that if you keep getting the same feedback there is a chance you might want to take notice… because you are the common denominator!
- If you have decided this context is important enough, you could ask several people, so you can compare notes.
- Even if you are still wanting to reject the feedback of others you could ask yourself what it would mean to you if the feedback were true?

If you tend to rely on other people to know if you are doing a good job and/or you tend to take things personally (even when you know rationally that this is not their intention), remember that feedback is data. It may sometimes feel personal, but it is simply someone else's perspective. One person's feedback (even your partner's), is no more valid than your own.

As with all feedback, you will need to decide for yourself whether you think the feedback from

Key Pointer

Whose problem is it anyway?
- If many people have a problem with the way you do something, then it may be **your** problem.
- If one person has a problem with the way you do something, it may be **their** problem.
- If that person is your partner, then it may be a problem for **both of you** and probably needs to be addressed in some way, shape or form.

your partner is something you can and will do something about. If you are not prepared to change, then the conversation that transpires may lead you to chapter 8.

Making and Taking Apologies

<u>Saying sorry</u>

Why is sorry so hard to say? It does seem to depend on one's culture. The British, for example, are renowned for saying 'sorry' (often with no meaning), but how about when it really counts?

Perhaps some people are afraid to say sorry because it makes them vulnerable. If we have said something destructive to our partner (spoken in anger perhaps), to say sorry could be deemed an admission of guilt, fault weakness and/or wrongdoing.

A retreating energy may find it hard to express an apology out loud. An 'internally referenced' person may not think they have anything to apologise for. Despite the fact that some people seem incapable or reluctant to say sorry when it comes to relationship slip-ups, it is interesting, that on the whole, there is greater credibility in a meaningful apology than in no apology at all. Rather than demonstrate weakness, a heart-felt and vulnerable apology can be the most courageous act.

However, what if you feel genuinely that you have done nothing wrong and so have nothing to apologise for? If your partner is upset, angry or unhappy with you, it is still useful to understand why. Ask for more information (e.g. "I'm not sure yet what you are angry about. What's happened?"). Seek to understand their perspective. What do they need from you? Are you able/willing to do anything about that? For further guidance here, see Chapter 8.

Of course, an advancing energy might apologise a lot, particularly if they are 'externally referenced' too. There is a risk here that the over-apologising could become 'white noise' and so get tuned out when it really matters. The 'sorry' carries less meaning and impact.

From a balanced-constructive perspective, perhaps the most important thing when apologising, is to really mean it (rather than using it defensively to 'fob off' our partner). Then after the initial apology, comes a willingness to put things right and to take action accordingly.

<u>Accepting an apology</u>

The other side of saying sorry, of course, is the ability to graciously accept an apology from your partner. This would mean to hear their apology without interrupting them, to acknowledge what they've said and then find a way to forgive and let it go. To be **balanced constructive** would also mean not using it later as a weapon or bringing it up to attack/defend at a later point. It would also mean 'not going on about it' when and after the heartfelt apology has been made!

If you feel you cannot forgive your partner, this would imply that either what they have done is a serious breach to your agreed boundaries and ground-rules or it is another example in a sequence of *minor misdemeanours* (and 'sorry' doesn't cut it anymore). This may be a more serious matter in the status of the relationship. Is this something you can try to resolve through discussion and resetting boundaries or do you need external help? Worst case scenario, is this a sign of an unworkable relationship? (If so, see chapter 8.)

Communication, Communication, Communication

Whether it is helping the relation-ship stay afloat or keeping the tunnel clear between you, communication is the key. Whatever metaphor (mixed or otherwise) you choose to use when it comes to communication, we know it is essential and we know what happens when communication breaks down.

Chapter 8

Relating Through Difference

"It is not our differences that divide us.
It is our inability to recognize, accept, and celebrate those differences."
Audre Lorde, *Our Dead Behind Us: Poems*

In This Chapter...

In this chapter we will help you understand how to identify and handle differences in your relationship. The ability to relate and work through differences is one of the fundamental skills of effective and healthy couples.

We will be exploring the following questions:

- What is a 'difference'?
- Why do people try and change their partner?
- What can you do about 'unacceptable differences'?
- What is the consequence of continued conflict?
- How might you take a **balanced-constructive** approach?
- What are some practical steps to handling differences?

What's in a Difference?

A relationship tends to be easier where we are similar and in harmony! However, the true test of a relationship is the ability to continue relating to one another when we *don't* agree with what our partner wants or says.

In relationship, we consider there to be two interconnected types of difference:

- *Wanting our partner to be different*: Perhaps there is something that we do not like about our partner, something that irritates or upsets us. It might be an attitude or a behaviour, in the way they treat us or other people. This trait may have existed from the start of the relationship; we might have ignored it or it may not have risen to the surface. Alternatively, the trait may have developed over time.
- *Having a difference of values, opinions, needs, outcomes and approaches*: We are two different human beings and we may want different things. We may have different beliefs which manifest in day-to-day living. Again, some of these differences may have been there since we met our partner but we tolerated them in the 'honeymoon' phase. Alternatively, it could be that we are drifting in different directions in terms of what we want in life.

We will begin the chapter with a brief exploration of the 'difference mindset', including the thought patterns that create differences (**destructive/unbalanced**) in couples or resolve those differences (**balanced-constructive**). We will address the issue of one partner wanting the other to change and then when there is a difference of needs or approaches.

I want you to be different: If you loved me you would change!

There is a curious aspect to romantic relationships that we are sure you will have seen, experienced or perhaps been 'guilty' of yourself: this is the drive to get our partner to change! Indeed, we sometimes see people who want to change the very thing they were most attracted to in the beginning of the relationship!

A Case In Point

We have worked with a number of couples who were apparently falling out of love with one another. In some instances, the very thing that attracted them to their partner was now becoming an irritator (i.e. the thing they now wanted to change).

For example, one woman who was once attracted to the strong, powerful side of her partner now wanted him to be vulnerable and share his feelings. In another couple, the man who once liked his partner's ability to chat to anyone, now wanted her to "shut up"!

Why might we do this?

1) Trying to fix the past through the present

Earlier we wrote about how we model ourselves on our same sex parent (usually) and are attracted to people who in some way represent our opposite sex parent. This is just the beginning of the journey. Once in relationship we begin to look at things differently. We are attracted to a person who fits our internal pattern or map of what an 'appropriate partner' looks, sounds and feels like. Just because we are attracted to this pattern does not mean that it brings us happiness and satisfaction; it may simply be known and 'familiar'!

Once in relationship we may set about trying to change aspects of the relationship that are unsatisfying. We think we are in the 'here and now' but we are deluding ourselves. What we are really trying to do is fix what was wrong with the relationship we had with our parent(s) (or saw *between* our parents) during our childhood.

2) Seeking fairness and equity

Another explanation links to something called 'equity theory'[27], which suggests that we require and desire a sense of *fairness* in our relationships; we feel more comfortable if we are being treated equitably. When a relationship starts to feel out of balance for any reason there is a sense of discomfort in the partner who feels the unfairness. This is likely to be an unconscious realisation that may then manifest into a feeling that we are being taken advantage of.

> **A Case In Point**
>
> Imagine someone is attracted to a partner for their laid back and fun attitude to life. In the early days of the relationship this quality may seem attractive and admirable. However, as the relationship progresses beyond the honeymoon phase, this trait starts to be perceived differently. Perhaps there is a sense that their partner is now irresponsible, leaving all the hard decisions to them while their partner has all the fun.

3) Realising the 'dark side'

A further explanation might come from 'social exchange theory'[27] where we begin to see the 'dark side' of some of our partner's traits, including those that were once (and may still be) attractive. It is also possible that we might still like (or be comfortable with) this trait in other people but become annoyed with it in our partner! Why would this be? Simply put, with others, we can leave the party and go home. With our partner, not only are they there at the party, but they are there at home as well. The issue here is perhaps 'over-exposure' to our partner.

We can look at all traits and behaviours from two sides. Each will have a positive 'light' side and negative 'dark' side. It all depends how we view it. Consider admiring a person for being a hard-worker; later that same trait seems to have transformed into 'workaholic'. Their behaviour may not have changed, but our perspective and reaction to them has. Perhaps we have been 'overexposed' to that trait so it now begins to appear unattractive.

Have a look at the list of traits below. In the first column, there are examples of things people might put on their 'wish-list' when they are seeking a partner in the first place. Then, consider the advantages ('light side') and potential disadvantages ('dark side') of each trait:

Trait	Advantages	Disadvantages
Light-hearted	*e.g. easy going*	*e.g. not taking things seriously*
Independent	*e.g. strong, self-reliant*	*e.g. unavailable*
Fun		
Clever		
Attentive		
Practical		
World-wise		

What if the issue is not that our partner has changed, but that we have begun to see them in a different light?

<u>What can we do about it?</u>

Unsurprisingly the solution begins with self-awareness; where a couple realise what is happening, there is the opportunity to change their reactions. The steps are straightforward:

1. Recognise that what is annoying you may be connected to what first attracted you to your partner.
2. Remind yourself why you were attracted to this trait and reframe your new reactions more positively.
3. Identify your *own* traits. Understand how they may be perceived by your partner and increase your awareness of the dark side of your own traits.
4. Share new experiences with your partner regularly (to give you both counters to each of your own habitual behaviours).

These steps are certainly a great place to start in terms of understanding and perhaps accepting our partner's traits. Now let us look at ideas for potentially extinguishing the annoyance:

- If we liked it at the beginning, how can we continue to like it now?

- If we were *really* to communicate with each other, what would happen?
- If we examine our own habitual behaviours and find them change worthy, why not just change them?
- Is it possible to be truly accepting of others? Can we let ourselves and our partner 'off the hook'?
- What would happen if we lived our relationship in the present?

Are there unacceptable differences?

In a relationship there may be (a) differences we *find hard* to accept, (b) differences we *cannot* accept and (c) differences we *will not* accept. This may range from 'irritators' to 'serious issues':

- Irritators are things that challenge our boundaries, but don't necessarily cross the line, for example: leaving toenail clippings on the floor, not putting the washing-up liquid away in the cupboard, leaving dishes on top of the dishwasher, leaving lights on or drawers open.
- Serious issues might be something that crosses the line of our boundaries, hence becoming a 'deal-breaker'. For example: infidelity, verbal or physical abuse, illegal/immoral activities. The examples here are meant to be generic but deal-breakers would be specific to each couple (i.e. what they decide).

There may be (what we would call) an 'ecology' issue here. We, as a couple, believe that if one partner does something purposefully that might endanger the other (physically, mentally, legally), this would usually fit into the category of 'unacceptable' and may result in the ending of the relationship.

Alternatively, if a couple are finding that there are *too many* 'irritators' for them to accept or respect their partner, this too could ultimately result in the ending of the relationship. However, we would first recommend that the couple try some form of third-party mediation or couples therapy first. We might consider this the 'Balanced-Constructive exit', i.e. *either you work out your relationship differences* or *you work your way out of the relationship.*

If the differences are truly irreconcilable, then get individual help to avoid repeating the same issues in future relationships! If possible, take time in between one relationship and another to establish what didn't work and what you might do differently in the future, particularly in terms of partner choice, boundary setting at the start and behaviours that may be more effective.

When we still love our partner, and want to stay with them, but still find there are irritators that are too hard to accept, here are some ideas:

- Do some personal development. This is not meant to be a flippant statement. When a person lets go of some of their *own* baggage, they tend to find it easier to tolerate other people. Remember that irritators (i.e. things that we get irritated about) are simply the retriggering/restimulation of our own 'stuff'. For more on this, go back to chapter 5.
- Consider: How much of an issue is this in comparison to your overall relationship? In honesty, are you blowing this out of proportion?
- Look your partner in the eyes[28] and remember why you fell in love with them and why you love them now. If they are not around, imagine them at their most attractive, e.g. gazing at you lovingly or smiling.
- Have a read of the next segment…

What you focus on is what you get!

Imagine a screen where one half is dirty and the other half is clean. Which side would you prefer to look through at the world and at your partner? Imagine this screen is in your mind and you have a choice which side you perceive the world (and/or your partner) through. We call this model, the Windscreen of Perception:

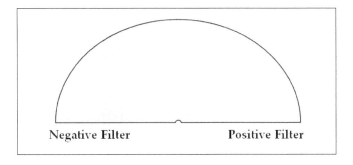

If we consider the 'world out there' for a moment, do bad things happen? Yes, of course. And do good things happen. Again, yes of course. Indeed, we could say that there is a continuum of very bad to very good... and we could come up with examples all the way along that line. If someone thinks the world is a bad and dangerous place, they can find evidence for this. If someone else thinks the world is a good and amazing place, they can find evidence for this too. It is not actually about the world out there! Our experience of the world is determined by the filter we use to look at it. Wherever we look, we will find evidence for our own particular filter. The philosophy here would be: focus on the 'light side', be aware of the 'dark side' and change/influence what you can but accept what you simply cannot change.

The same is true for how we see our partner (and indeed how we perceive our own self). If someone's view of their partner and the relationship had become muddied, they will find evidence for what is wrong. On the contrary, when someone is happy in their relationship, they will be looking through a cleaner filter and seeing the evidence. It is a self-fulfilling prophecy that supports whichever view we have.

What you focus on is what you see... what you see determines how you feel and what you experience.

In the same way that we cannot control the world out there, we cannot *control* our partner (though many try!) What we <u>can</u> control however is *what we focus on*. You are responsible for your filters!

We are *not* talking about being blind to destructive and disrespectful behaviours however. If you are interested in how successful couples think: Focus on the positive, be aware of the negative and communicate: (a) for more of the positive, tell your partner what you like, love, appreciate and admire, (b) for less of the negative, give your partner loving feedback and be clear about your boundaries (what is and is not okay for you). We will explore this further, later in the chapter.

When you focus on the positive aspects of your partner, the irritations are easier to accept and 'overlook'. Indeed, they may become endearing! In the film 'Good Will Hunting', a most poignant moment is when Robin Williams' character reveals that after his wife died, the things he missed the most were the very things that irritated him when she was alive; it was part of what made her 'her'.

The Unbalanced-Destructive relationship and the consequences of continued conflict

An **unbalanced-destructive** couple will usually have the mindset of *'either-or'*, for example: me or you, my way or your way, right or wrong, good or bad. The *either-or* mindset means only one of us can 'win' (e.g. an argument). This mindset can make it harder to find common ground or agreement with our partner when there is difference between us.

Consider the advancing-retreating dynamic in the face of difference. The advancing energy is likely to push for a resolution, to the point of not letting it go nor giving their partner space to talk. The retreating energy won't open up about the difference/disagreement/ conflict nor actively pursue a discussion/resolution.

Earlier, we explored the layers of constructive and destructive behaviours. It is perhaps obvious to see that destructive behaviours of avoidance, apprehension, antagonism and aversion (or in Gottman's 'four horsemen' model: stonewalling, defensiveness, criticism and contempt) have the potential to maintain and/or escalate conflict in a relationship.

If the 'four horsemen' are in place, there appears to be a degree of 'learned helplessness' that may set in which creates a new level of stonewalling and avoidance. Here, either one of the couple will tend to avoid issues by shutting down completely or leaving the scene. It is as if they are caught in a double-bind of 'damned if I say anything, damned if I don't'. And so, the couple move from *difference* to *indifference*.

The point of *indifference* is where a couple cease to care about each other as they used to. They are less and less bothered about resolving their issues and may begin to look elsewhere for comfort and engagement.

In simple terms, in the face of *difference*, the Four Horsemen of the Apocalypse tend to ride in when the couple can *only* see the *negatives* of each other's perspectives/personality. And so, they spiral down through argument, conflict, indifference and then perhaps separation.

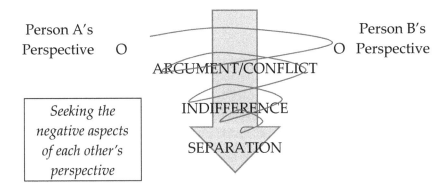

A moment of Unbalanced-Destructive behaviour: When the Graces are forgotten

What if a couple are in the middle of an argument and temporarily forget the Five Relationship Graces in their anger? It is relatively natural for an arguing couple to put up barriers and disregard previous agreements, however, **the Graces are still there for them to return to afterwards**. It is better that they can refocus on something constructive than flounder in miscommunication.

If you believe that you will reject the Graces in the heat of an argument consider:
   (a) how important is your relationship?
   (b) are you prepared to develop as a human being and to become more emotionally mature?

Of course, if either partner decides to permanently reject their agreements, this may be an indicator of a mal-functioning relationship (and this is something we will discuss later). To reject the agreements is both counter-productive and self-destructive because it opens the door for your partner to follow suit. It is the Graces that hold us above and beyond such destructive behaviours.

With personal awareness and emotional maturity, a couple can return to the agreements more quickly. Indeed, they may even develop the skills of observing themselves, stepping back from high emotions and staying with the Graces. They are then in a position to 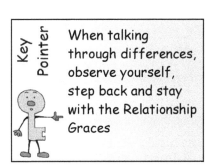 help their partner return to the Graces (indeed, it is hard to continue conflicting with someone when they are not conflicting back!)

Key Pointer: When talking through differences, observe yourself, step back and stay with the Relationship Graces

A Balanced-Constructive Approach

The **balanced-constructive** couple tend to have an alternative mindset to those that focus on each other's negatives. Their focus is 'both-and', for example: me and you, your way and my way, both right, both have right and wrong! The both-and mindset means that we always seek a 'win-win', i.e. what is good about both of our ideas/approaches/styles and how can we find a way that gives us the 'best of both worlds'?

When a couple are moving through the constructive layers, they tend to carry the following beliefs about *difference*:

Layer	Beliefs
+1 Awareness	• "There is/appears to be difference" • "I understand we are different" • "I acknowledge our difference" • "I acknowledge *you* in the ways you are different to me"
+2 Acceptance	• "Difference is okay/good" • "I accept we are different" • "I accept our differences" • "I accept *you* in the ways you are different to me"
+3 Appreciation	• "Difference can be useful" • "I appreciate (am thankful) we are different" • "I appreciate our differences" • "I appreciate *you* in the ways you are different to me"
+4 Admiration	• "Difference is the potential for excellence" • "I admire that we are different" • "I admire our differences" • "I admire *you* in the ways you are different to me" • "As a united couple, our differences make us stronger and more resourceful in life"

Successful couples seek the positive in one other and in each other's positions, perspectives and personality. When faced with difference they seek synthesis and synergy and by doing so spiral upwards through innovation, connectedness and unity.

According to Michael Hall[29], synergy is part of the *self-actualisation* process. As we *self-actualise*, distinctions and differences disappear. The relationship becomes greater than the sum of its parts and together, we can achieve things we could never have achieved independently.

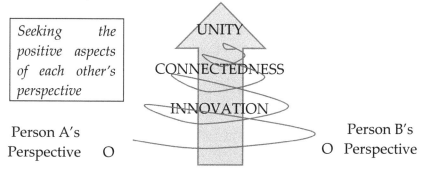

On one level, it is as simple as this... when we see the negatives/ disadvantages of each other's position, we will likely fall into conflict. When we see the positives/advantages, we transcend from difference into innovation and connection.

We might consider a **balanced-constructive** relationship one in which couples will talk about their partner in constructive ways, openly discussing what they appreciate and admire (both when with their partner and when their partner is not there). How many couples do you know who do this? As long as this is done with an awareness of the audience (i.e. not overly sycophantic!) it provides a refreshing change from those who moan about their supposed loved ones.

Listen to yourself when you talk to and about your partner. Notice your body language when you are with them. As long as it is ecological to do so (i.e. doesn't harm you or others in any way), seek to find the positives in who they are, what they do and what they want. What do you appreciate in your partner? What do you admire about them?

And, of course, remember to tell them from time to time!

Practical steps to handling differences

So far in this chapter, we have explored the nature of differences, how they happen and the mindset of both unbalanced-destructive and balanced-constructive. Now we want to outline some practical steps you can take to resolve differences of:

- Beliefs and opinions
- Values
- Ideas and solutions
- Needs and outcomes
- Expectations

General principles

For all of the guides below, as well as the Five Relationship Graces, there are some general principles and behaviours that are good practice to apply:

- Remember at all times that *you are on the same side*.
- Seek to hold a constructive internal image of your partner (e.g. that they are resourceful, loving and loveable).
- Be prepared to get clear about what they *really* want. Listen to your partner's position and seek the positive intentions (the benefits, why they want what they want): What would they get by achieving their outcome?

- Reflect the positive aspects back to them (in part to demonstrate understanding).
- Be clear about what *you* really want. Put forward your position and the positive intentions (benefits) of your own position: What would you get by achieving your outcome?
- Stay '**balanced**'. Avoid pushing your own opinion, ideas, needs, expectations on your partner. Alternatively, avoid clamming up and not saying anything. Be prepared to listen and empathise with them *and* express your own side.
- Stay '**constructive**'. Hold the frame of awareness and acceptance throughout, staying open to possibilities and discovery. Remember what you appreciate and admire about your partner (even if you don't currently agree with what they are saying).
- Take a joint problem-solving approach, *working together* on the issue (rather than on opposing sides). Seek solutions that genuinely work for both you and your partner (rather than trying to make one side better than the other).

<u>Handling a difference of beliefs and opinions</u>

Opinions could be defined as stated/expressed beliefs. If handled poorly, different beliefs about important matters can be detrimental to a couple; so how might we hold different beliefs and opinions and yet remain balanced-constructive?

When handling other people's beliefs, even if they contradict your own, remember that no-one owns the ultimate truth! Whilst they may be true to the individual, beliefs hold no objective 'truth value'. Beliefs are personal.

Assuming that your partner's opinions are not threatening to your safety and wellbeing, the following steps are designed to create or maintain *balance* in your relationship:

1. Be open to the fact that your partner believes something other than you do. If they state an opinion you might say something like: "I hadn't considered that perspective" or "I didn't know you believed that" or "that's an interesting way of looking at it."
2. Ask for more information: "Tell me more about why you believe that."
3. Seek anything you can agree with and say so.
4. Once you have heard their opinion, decide if you want to state your own: "I have a different perspective…" or "the way I see it is…" If it is a case of them having a different memory of an event: "My experience/memory of that was different…"

The idea here is to keep it away from the level of right and wrong, true or false. As soon as we think we are right, we become positional.

Handling a difference of values

What is important to you and to your partner? It is quite possible that different things are important and this needs to be acknowledged and expressed.

Contravened values (i.e. where someone behaves in a manner that is contrary to your values) often result in anger. Hence it is useful to understand both your own and your partner's values in a given context.

One way of identifying some of your values is through what angers you (even mildly):

Steps to identifying Values	Example 1	Example 2
1) Consider a behaviour that irritates or annoys you.	Lateness	Not listening

2) When someone is *doing* that behaviour, what are they *being* (i.e. what quality are they exhibiting)?	Disrespectful, Inconsiderate, Unreliable.	Disrespectful, Unfair, Closed.
3) Identify the opposite/counter of that quality (from your perspective)? How would you like them to be?	Respectful, Considerate, Reliable.	Respectful, Fair, Open.
4) The counter to the annoying quality is likely to be linked to your values. "I value..."	Respect, Consideration, Reliability.	Respect, Fairness, Openness.

When talking through a difference of values:

1. Ask for more information ("tell me more about what's important to you about this" and if necessary, to explore further: "and to help me understand, when you have that, what does it give you?"),
2. Seek any agreement ("that's important to me too") or empathy ("I get that x,y,z are important to you"),
3. Decide what you can accept (or tolerate) in your partner's value set and what still needs to be resolved (remember you can love a person even if you don't share or love all of their values),
4. Express what is important to you,
5. Seek a way (or ways) forward that gives you both what is important to you. Practical solutions may involve doing some things separately and others things together.

Handling a difference of ideas and solutions

A simple thing that you can do when talking about a difference of ideas and solutions is:

1. Ask for more information ("tell me more about your idea"),
2. Consider any detail that is good about their idea and how it might help the current situation. Reflect back and tell them what you like about their idea: "What I like about your idea is that it gives us..."
3. Then express your idea clearly including what you believe it gives you and your partner (i.e. the benefits of your idea/how it helps resolve the current situation),
4. Use the benefits of both ideas to start a conversation about what you might do to get the benefits of both of your ideas. Be prepared to look at a 'third way', an alternative solution that you can both be happy with.

Handling a difference of needs and outcomes

Where there is a difference of needs and outcomes:

1. Ask them to tell you more about the situation and most importantly, what they need ("what do you need from me/the situation?")
2. Summarise/repeat back to them what you have heard them say,
3. Then tell them what you need from them/the situation,
4. Using the combined needs of you and your partner, discuss ideas/solutions that will meet those needs.

Handling a difference of expectations

In chapter 6, we discussed the concept of boundaries and expectations. What do you and your partner want and expect from one another? What kind of behaviours would cross the line?

In addition, we might have expectations of events and things that need to be discussed, particularly where we discover a difference in what we are seeking. A classic example here might be about a holiday, where one partner wants one thing and the other wants something else.

There is a tool, developed by Robert Dilts[30], which provides a useful process for any couple that encounters a difference they have yet to resolve. This process is called the NLP Negotiation Model and whilst we have adapted it somewhat, the philosophy behind it fits our other 'handling difference' approaches.

If, as a couple, you encounter a difference in expectations, you will first of all need to agree that *you both want to resolve it*. Once you have agreed, you have your first (and perhaps greatest) point of common ground. Now that you have a joint purpose, give yourself time to work through the following questions:

1. First establish what your current disagreement is about. Also, what, if anything, do you agree about?
   For example, if the topic is a holiday, is it the type of holiday and/or the location?
2. "What specifically do you want in this context?" When you have both answered this question, establish the 'why' (i.e. for what purpose) for your responses: "I want X, in order to Y". Make sure you both understand the desired outcomes and purpose of what your partner wants (even if you don't currently agree with them).
   In the holiday example, perhaps one partner wants a beach holiday in order to relax and the other partner wants an adventure holiday in order to have fun and explore.
3. For each of your responses, ask yourselves: "What would having that give you?" You and your partner then share what you will get by achieving what you want. If there is still a gap, you would take your new responses and ask the question

again ("and what would having *that* give you?") until you find a similar answer to one another. In this way you are seeking a higher level of common ground.

For the couple planning their holiday, perhaps something that both partners ultimately want is a place where they can both 'recharge their batteries'.

4. "How might we both get what we ultimately want?" You can now begin to sort out the details through 'trading' ("*if I give you some of what you want, then you give me some of what I want*") and creative problem solving. If, at any stage, there is disagreement again, return back to a recent agreement and work from there.

The holiday couple might seek a place that can meet the needs of both and then trade a little.... or they may find another solution. A couple we know go on holiday with friends and spend some days going in different directions. They come back together later in the day and have interesting things to share over a meal and glass of wine!

Conclusions

In each of the approaches to handling difference, the overarching method is the same: find out what both of you want, find out what you would each get by having what you want and then seek a third path that meets your 'positive intentions'.

Difference itself is neither good nor bad… it is our *approach to handling* difference that will determine whether it becomes constructive (innovating, unifying and bonding) or destructive (conflicting, upsetting and hurting).

The extent to which we can be comfortable with difference and able to handle it, will most probably determine the making or breaking of our relationships.

Chapter 9

Revivifying Relationships

(How to Re-engage with the Honeymoon Phase)

"After the fire, the fire still burns."
Pete Townshend/Roger Daltrey, *"After the Fire"*

"Having their fling again,
younger than spring again,
feeling that zing again, wow!"
Perry Como, *"Papa Loves Mambo"*

In This Chapter...

In this chapter we will examine the 'honeymoon phase' of a relationship and what happens after. We will introduce some ideas on how to rekindle the flame.

We will be exploring the following questions:
- How do we fall in love?
- What would an unbalanced 'Honeymoon Phase' be like?
- How can you build a Balanced-Constructive relationship?
- What happens when the Honeymoon phase is over?
- How can you fall in love again?

How did you meet?

A Case In Point

Imagine the scene.... A group of people are sitting around a large kitchen table eating breakfast. A pretty woman sits at one end of the table talking to her friend. "Now, I'm looking for a knight in shining armour," she sighs. A young man sitting at the other end of the table looks up and says to her: "I've always considered myself to be the knight in shining armour." As their eyes meet, the table seems to concertina and everyone else in the room disappears...

Ten days later, her Decree Absolute arrives (for she had been married before), and he sends her a card with a picture of a knight in shining armour gazing into the loving eyes of a maiden on a horse. Inside the card he writes simply: "To my Unchained Melody".

We both love stories of how couples met. These stories range from the romantic to the 'coincidental' to the 'silly but cute' to the somewhat awkward and some even begin with: "I couldn't stand them when we first met!" In films and television, this is known as the *'meet cute'*.

- How did *you* and your partner meet?
- What is your story?
- What do you tell others and how do you tell it?

The stories of how we met our partner can grow and develop over time; some become sillier, funnier or even more romantic. Our meeting story becomes part of our mythology; it is, in a sense, our 'creation' myth and can be an important part of our joint identity as a couple.

My grandparents, Bert and Minnie had known each other for a little while as children when they both lived in Derbyshire. Time moved on and my Grandpa moved back to London. Nana had trained as a nurse and had been offered a job at a hospital in Surrey. Their parents were still in touch, so Grandpa was asked to escort Nana across London from one station to another. And so, they met again in the mid-1920s, under the clock at St Pancras Station. By the time they arrived at Waterloo Station, they had fallen in love.

Joe

Falling in Love... The Honeymoon Phase

In the early days of a relationship, we tend to experience a very rich and intense level of interaction, this is what we mean when we say the *honeymoon phase*. We are not necessarily talking about the formality of marriage here; indeed, for many couples, by the time (and if) they get married, the relationship's honeymoon phase may have long passed!

The honeymoon phase can last for weeks, months or even a couple of years. This is a normal part of the process of relationship building; we are forging bonds that will last through the years.

There is an intensity to this phase that would be exhausting to maintain forever. It would also likely lead to the exclusion of friends and family. It is healthy and natural to move through and then on from this stage.

The Oxytocin Effect

This 'honeymoon' bonding process is not just emotional and psychological, it is also chemical. The intensity of our interactions releases hormones particularly oxytocin often called the "cuddle chemical". Oxytocin is thought to promote trust, empathy and connection. Often couples withdraw into a unit, excluding others somewhat during this stage. They will often want to spend time together rather than in larger social gatherings during the honeymoon phase.

The exclusion of others outside the relationship might simply be a normal part of the early process, however at extreme it could create limitations in other parts of life ongoing… jobs still need to be attended and friends and family might need a wave from time to time! In contrast, some couples find (even in the early days) that the only way of relating to each other is if they are socialising in the company of friends. Sadly, if a couple struggle to feel comfortable alone together, we might question their chances in the long run. 'Honeymooners' won't always exclude others, of course. Many couples are able to balance their alone time with life outside.

Oxytocin may also have a 'dark side' which results in destructive behaviours. These behaviours may manifest in relationships where *passion* is defined as extreme jealousy, emotive argument and intense physical making up. For some people this may seem to work, however we would suggest that in a truly loving relationship, disagreement can be handled differently. It is worth noting here that if the honeymoon phase is full of pain and upset, the chances are that the pattern will continue beyond the honeymoon phase. If the honeymoon phase is not wonderful, then hear warning bells! Early unbalanced and/or destructive behaviours will likely be an indicator for the future.

Advancing and Retreating in the Honeymoon phase

An intense relationship at the start would suggest both partners advancing. This might be considered normal when the energies are relatively equal. Both parties might appear to others as a bit obsessive; they might be retreating from other relationships as they advance to their new-found love interest. Classic 'symptoms' of love manifest at this point, where neither partner can focus on other issues (such as work) because they have only one thing on their mind.

However, a relationship that begins with *unbalanced* energies is likely to continue that way (at least, without some form of intervention). If one partner withdraws in the early days (e.g. is often unavailable or doesn't return calls, emails or texts) this is a probable indicator of later behaviours. The same is true of the advancing energy (e.g. contacting their new partner at every possible moment or expressing 'I-love-you's within hours of meeting).

Balanced-Constructive behaviours: Building a new world

When we first meet someone and get to know them, we are being introduced into their private world. We get to see and experience things about them that they do not share with everyone. We see how they live and how they decorate their space. We see the 'nick-nacks' and personal mementos they have accumulated before they met us. We are privy to their memories and nostalgia. We listen to the music they like, watch the movies they love.

Here we discover a fully formed 'other world', a lifetime that has been led by someone else… suddenly we are reminded on the most fundamental level that someone else *really exists*. We are not alone in having a rich tapestry of history, emotions and thoughts. In the words of Tigger: "I found somebody just like me… and I thought I was the only one of them."

This is the point in our new relationship where we seek and discover more and more of what we both like and what we have in common.

The fire alights

The beginning of a relationship could be termed 'intense-multisensory'. The internal image we hold of our new beau will often be described as colourful, bright, vibrant, focussed, close-up, harmonic, buzzing and fizzy. Some of these things may ring bells for you and you will no doubt be able to add some more of your own.

To continue the multisensory theme, we will tend to throw everything we have at building the attraction. It has been suggested in the field of NLP that we have 'love strategies'[31]. Love strategies are the 'giving and receiving' behaviours we use to gain and maintain a relationship. Not only do we *do* some of these behaviours, we also *like to experience* them from our partner. Everyone has their own unique preferences, but the rule of thumb is that we tend to *give* in the manner that we like to *receive*.

Imagine someone at the beginning of a relationship. If they are keen, they will tend to use a multisensory approach (regardless of their personal preferences); they are likely use all sensory channels (visual, auditory/hearing, kinaesthetic/feeling, olfactory/smell and gustatory/taste)! For example:

Visual:	• Look attractive, dress to impress • Show how much we like them • Give gifts and flowers • Send cute pictures • Take pictures together
Auditory:	• Listen to music – create an 'our tune' • Write poetry and read it to them! • Say sweet/romantic things, whisper sweet nothings • Give compliments • Speak with a soft and pleasing tone
Kinaesthetic:	• Touch, hug, cuddle, kiss etc. • Make love more frequently • Make them feel good • Offer them a jacket/coat on a cold night
Olfactory:	• Shower regularly (!) and smell good • Wear perfume / aftershave • Avoid breaking wind in their company!

Gustatory:	• Go out for meals, share food
	• Cook for one another, cook together
	• Share a bottle of wine
	• Open a box of chocolates

Of course, not everybody will use all of the examples above, but you no doubt get the idea. Sustaining this level of intensity for any great length of time could be exhausting and so most relationships begin to settle. At this point, we may begin to revert to our own preferences and 'norms'.

Have a look at the list above and consider: which of these did you do as a couple when you first met and which do you do now? Feel free to add more examples!

After the Fire: What next?

In an ideal relationship, when the fire of the honeymoon phase dies down, the embers continue with a warm glow. However, we also need to understand some of the less constructive behaviours that may appear at this point. By knowing some of the warning signs, we can seek to prevent destructive elements creeping in. By being able to spot them happening, we can take action to resolve them rather than allow them to take hold and fester.

Destructive elements and Constructive solutions

Please note that these are not things that *will* happen in relationships, they are simply based on observations we have made where some relationships have struggled to continue. We want you to be aware of these things to make sure they don't creep into your own relationship.

Many couples never experience these kinds of challenges; however, there are plenty of couples that do. So, what can we do if we realise we are not where we want to be? How can we *thrive* (not just survive) beyond the honeymoon phase?

Destructive Elements	Constructive Solutions
Normalising to the point of neutralising It seems that after the Honeymoon phase, many couples begin to normalise and habituate to their partner. They find less new and exciting things to discover and perhaps they begin to take their partner for granted. Feelings become 'flatter' and less intense, the brightness fades and their partner seems to blend into the background of life. There are some people who are addicted to the honeymoon phase of the relationship. For them the fading of this phase results in them leaving the relationship and looking for someone new to get that buzz with all over again.	*Get interested together* Observe and listen to your partner. What do they like/love? Imagine you want to buy them a present that they would adore. What would you need to know in order to do that? Be interested in their interests even if it is not really your thing. Enjoy the fact that they enjoy it! Have your own interests too. Most importantly, find or create shared interests. Go places together, do things together. Get creative. Discover things you can both look forward to and get genuinely excited about. If 'new' things engage you, go out and do new things together!
Associating with other relationships For some, the 'internal pictures' of their loved one may become generalised and sit in a category along with other relationships. Their internal model then becomes contaminated with the hurts of other less successful relationships; unfavourable comparisons are made with previous partners. We	*Disassociate from old relationships* The only comparison should be to ask what is *better* about my current relationship? What do you have now that you didn't have before? What does your partner bring to the relationship? What have they got that others didn't? And what do *you* bring to the relationship to make it better?

may begin perceiving our partner as having traits similar to a previous partner. This may be due to unconscious distorting and filtering and may not actually relate to our current partner at all.	
Reverting to type After the honeymoon phase, we may begin to revert to our 'normal' level of expressing love. This will probably be based on our own preferences, i.e. we give love in the way we'd like to receive it. In other words, we only use our own *love strategies*[31].	*Remember your partner!* Be smart here. Watch your partner, listen to your partner. What do they do to offer their love to you? Try reflecting their style back to them (and/or ask them what they want). Be prepared to ask kindly for what you want too! (See later in this chapter for more details!)
Finding fault and irritation Some of the things our partner did in the early days, we tolerated, overlooked or perhaps even found endearing. Now, however, they become irritating. Our partner is not fulfilling our 'internal representation' of what a proper partner should be. One partner may begin to think their 'loved one' is incapable in some way and so no longer trusts them. They give their partner detailed lists of what to do. They feel consistently let down by their partner and so take a tighter control of the reins. Perhaps they start treating their partner like a child, assuming a parental role in buying their clothes, telling them how to	*Find acceptance* What do you think your partner *should* do/be like? Now remember that 'should' indicates a *fantasy-reality gap*! When we say someone 'should' do/be something, we are often being *unreal*istic. No-one is perfect (and who said *our* version of perfection is the 'correct' or most important!) Express your needs to your partner but be prepared to accept them for who they are. The art of acceptance is also known as 'growing up'. Find ways to build trust in your partner. Be clear about your own needs but give them space to do their own thing, buy their own clothes, make their own decisions! Are you their partner or their parent? Remember they are not a

behave and ultimately disempowering them. On the contrary, instead of parenting, they may behave more childishly. Indeed, to be unable behave in an adult manner can be a symptom of the 'Little Prince/ Princess syndrome'[32]	child, so stop controlling them and let them be an adult!
Expecting our partner to be otherwise This has similarities to the previous issue, however in this scenario, we expect our partner to 'understand us by now'. We expect them to mind-read and know what we are thinking and what we want. We shouldn't have to tell them, they should know! If you hear yourself say: "If you loved me, you would…" you have slipped into this 'expectation' behaviour.	*Communicate in a balanced manner!* If you expect your partner to know what you are thinking, feeling and what you need, you are placing too much of a strain on the relationship. Talk to your partner. Go through the 'complementary contracting' questions in chapter 6. Discuss plans and agreements that you can both be happy about. Ask them for what you want. Check that they know what you need. Remember your partner may love you *even* if they if don't know what you are thinking!

In many of the examples above, couples begin to see the differences between them: differences in approach, in temperament, in what is acceptable. The trick is to resolve these differences before they become irreconcilable. If you find yourself noticing differences between you and your partner, consciously choose to remind yourself of what you have in common. Remember that no matter what life throws at you, *you are on the same side*. Steve Andreas[33] in *Transforming Your Self* suggests that conflict lies in comparison and seeking differences. The path to resolving these conflicts", he says, "is always to start focusing attention on the *similarities* that unite the two sides – noticing all the ways in which the two are the *same."*

For those couples who can develop a **balanced-constructive** approach as they move beyond the honeymoon phase, there is the potential to reap the rewards of a committed, trusting and rich relationship.

Revivifying and Reconnecting: Falling in Love again

Whilst it might not be completely healthy to wander around *forever* in a love-struck daze, what can we do to rekindle the fire and feel some of that spark and flame again?

The following ideas are things that you can do alone but even better *with* your partner.

Remember your partner's love strategy

As mentioned earlier in this chapter, 'love strategies' is an idea that came from the field of NLP[31]. A love strategy is the method(s) we use to feel and express love. During the honeymoon phase, when we are falling in love, we tend to put a fair amount of energy into fulfilling our partner's preferred love strategies by giving them something of everything! This might seem like hard work over a longer period of time so the idea here is to work smarter and not harder!

Rather than using your own love preferences as a template for your partner, what does your partner actually want? What do they say, what do they ask for and what do they do? How do they express love? The likelihood is: whatever way they *express* love is how they like to *receive* it. Talk with your partner; ask them what they like and how they know if they are really loved by you. Understand yourself and how you know *you* are feeling loved; let them know.

Consider the following questions:
- How do you know your partner loves you?
- How do you express love?
- How does your partner express love?
- How would your partner like to experience love from you?
- How would you like your partner to express love to you?

Review your internal pictures

Most of us carry a 'generalised' picture of our partner in our mind. We might call this image a 'template'. Even when our partner is not around physically, we still have them with us in our mind. This template, both content and quality of image, will affect how we *feel* about our partner when we think of them.

If we imagine them in a particular way, but this doesn't match how they *really* are, what happens? If someone has an out of date picture of their partner, they may find themselves disappointed when they see their partner in the real world. The next time you look at your partner, update your internal imagery to match the real world. Fall in love again with who your partner is *now*.

Consider the following questions:
- Imagine your partner in your mind's eye.
- How up to date is the picture?
- How do they look?
- What is their facial expression?
- What emotions or mood do they seem to be experiencing?
- How are they looking at you (indeed are they looking at you)?
- Does the picture feel good/right/comfortable? If not, make some changes (e.g. imagine them smiling and looking at you with a loving gaze) until you feel more connected and warm towards them.

When you imagine your partner, you will notice that they will be in a particular location. For example, they might be directly in front of you, or off to one side. They might be close up or a bit further away. It is interesting, isn't it, that even in our language we talk about a partner being 'distant' or that a couple are really 'close'. Lucas Derks[34] in *Social Panoramas* found that most people seem to hold loved ones close to them in their mind's eye, slightly to the left as if 'close to the heart'. If you find that your partner is not close, or that there are other people/things in the way, what might that mean to you? How might you feel about that? What if you brought them nearer so they are in front of any other people/things and at a close, comfortable proximity to you?

Consider the following questions:
- Imagine your partner
- Where is your partner in relation to you? If you were to point, where would they be?
- What size is your partner in the picture (e.g. are they normal size, small or 'larger than life')?
- Does their location feel good/right/comfortable? If not, move them closer/further, left or right until you feel more connected and warm towards them.

As well as location, we can also elicit (and where required, make changes to) many other qualities about the pictures we hold of our partner. In NLP, these qualities are known as 'sub-modalities'[35]. We can explore *what* internal pictures we hold of our partner but it is also important to understand *how* we hold them.

So, what are the *qualities* of the picture you hold of your partner? Go through the questions below and first notice, then make changes where you wish:

- Imagine your partner
- How bright is the picture?
- How colourful?
- Is the picture in focus... is your partner in focus?
- Is your partner in 3D or flat?

- Does your partner stand out from the background?
- Is the picture a video (moving) or a photo (still)?
- Are there any sounds? Is there music?
- Are there any feelings of movement?
- Are there any physical sensations?

Finally, imagine you and your partner together. How do you imagine that?

- Imagine a picture of you and your partner
- Are you both fully in the picture?
- Are you together or apart?
- What are you both doing in the picture?

A Case In Point

When imagining Melody and I together in the context of 'relationship', I imagine us in a slow-motion dance, holding hands and going around in a circle. We are both laughing and smiling. Music plays in the background – a drifting, haunting track by Brian Eno. There is a beautiful joy to this image accompanied by a tinge of sadness (that a lifetime is relatively brief and the dance cannot go on forever).

Joe

Replay your love story

We began this chapter with your 'meet cute', the story of how you met. Let us end where we began…

Think back for a moment to when you first met your partner. What is your love story? How did you meet? What happened? What attracted you to one other? If Hollywood was making a movie of those first moments, how would the world get to see it?

Then rewind back through the timeline of your relationship, stopping here and there at just the constructive, happy times. What are some of the loving things you have done together? What romantic occasions do you tell other people about? What are the 'together' moments you have shared that demonstrate you are loving companions on the curious journey of life? And if you have been thinking about these things, as you come to realise the present, what do you notice about you and your partner now? Take yourself into the future and create some time for play, for closeness, for exploration and for discovery together.

Take the time to reminisce fondly about what you have done.
Make the space to talk about the things you love about each other.
Create the moments to remember the good times.

After Word

We have been talking about writing a relationship book together for years! So why did it take us so long? The truth is, we almost didn't write it at all. We were concerned that if we wrote a book on relationships and then something happened so we parted company, wouldn't that look somewhat hypocritical and wouldn't that invalidate what we had written?

Why did we think that it was possible for us to part company? Did that mean we didn't really love each other? Of course not! Do we see a time when we might 'split up'? No, but do we think it is possible? Of course; we cannot predict the future. We have loved one another deeply and enjoyed each other's company for over 25 years. We have practiced what we 'preach' and we continue to explore 'best practice' together. We love each other now and we truly believe that we will love each other always.

However, we have also had conversations in the past about whether we could live without one another. The answer is yes. If something happened to either of us, or if we parted, we would be devastated of course. But we both know that we would pick ourselves up and live a happy life. Could we live apart? Yes. Do we want to? No.

We love being with one another and
we choose to live and thrive together!

Notes, Further Reading & References

Foreword

1. *Ecology*. The term 'ecology' as applied to the psychological and sociological realms was, as far as we know, introduced by Gregory Bateson. See Bateson, G. (2000) *Steps to an Ecology of Mind*, University of Chicago Press.

2. *Positive intentions*. The term 'positive intention' is used extensively in the field of neuro-linguistic programming (NLP) including its use in the 'presupposition' (empowering belief) that every behaviour has a positive intention [Dilts, R. (1983) *The Roots of NLP*, Meta publications]. It was probably introduced into the field by Virginia Satir. According to Steve Andreas: "One of the most powerful aspects of Virginia's work was her assumption that everyone's *intentions* were positive, no matter how horrible the behavior was..." [Andreas, S. (1991) *Virginia Satir: The Patterns of Her Magic* Real People Press (p.4)]

Introduction

3. *John Gottman and the Four Horsemen of the Apocalypse.* (See Gottman, J.M. (2007) *Why Marriages Succeed or Fail*, Bloomsbury.)

Chapter 1: The Dynamic Relationship

4. *Robin Norwood*. We recommend Robin Norwood's books: *Women Who Love Too Much* and *Why me? Why this? Why now?*

They were both written over twenty years ago but are still very relevant today.

Chapter 2: Balance, Attachment and Interdependence

5. *John Bowlby and attachment style*. See Bowlby J (1999) *Attachment. Attachment and Loss (vol. 1) (2nd ed.).* New York: Basic Books

   <u>Additional Notes</u>
   According to Bowlby attachment has an evolutionary component connected to our survival. The parenting style shapes the attachment style developed. Most developmental psychology books provide more information on this part of the theory if you want to know more. Below we have detailed the characteristics of each attachment style at the childhood stage:

   <u>Secure</u>
   - Confident and able to separate from parent.
   - Will seek comfort from parent when frightened
   - Receives positive emotional responses from parent on return.
   - Prefers parents to strangers

   <u>Ambivalent</u>
   - Often wary of strangers.
   - Become very distressed when parent leaves.
   - Do not appear to experience a sense of comfort from the parents return and may passively rejected the parent.

   <u>Avoidant</u>
   - May actively avoid their parents.
   - Will not seek out much comfort or contact from the parents.

- Shows little or even no preference between parents and strangers.

A fourth style has also been suggested that appears to be a mixture of ambivalent and avoidant called **"disorganised attachment".** This may develop where the parenting style is inconsistent and the child may feel both comforted and frightened of the parent at the same time.

In 1987, the researchers *Hazen and Shaver* [Hazan, C. and Shaver, P.R. (1987). Romantic love conceptualised as an attachment process. *Journal of Personality and Social Psychology*, 52(3), 511-524.] suggested that the attachment styles from childhood may form the basis of adult attachment styles in particular they noted that people with different attachment styles seemed to have specific patterns in their beliefs about love.

They noticed that securely attached adults were more likely to believe that romantic love was enduring while ambivalently attached adults reported falling in love often and avoidant types thought love was rare and/or temporary.

What we find interesting is the presence of such patterns; on the one hand we cannot say for sure that childhood attachment styles directly correlate with adult attachment styles but there does appear to be enough of a pattern to make this intriguing.

Secure Adults
When we start to look at the characteristics of adult attachment styles some interesting things start to surface. If we look first at securely attached adults, they are more likely to have good self-esteem and trusting long term relationships. They will share feelings with

friends and partners easily and comfortably. They will also feel comfortable seeking out social support.

They are most likely to be attracted to someone else who is also securely attached. These are the relationships that are most likely to be happy. From a psychological perspective, a happy relationship is a much higher experience of positive emotions than negative on a day to day basis.

Ambivalent Adults
There is some research that suggests that ambivalent attachment is relatively rare (e.g. 7 to 15% in infants), however when you read the characteristics we began to doubt that finding, at least in adults.

This style could be described as "needy" and the individual may spend a lot of time worrying that their partner may not love them. They become extremely distraught with the break-up of a relationship to a degree that could be described as obsessive.

Paradoxically they may also be reluctant to become close to others. So even though they fear their partner does not love them they may passively reject their partner. Descriptions of "clingy" and over-dependent are also given to this attachment style.

Avoidant Adults
The avoidant style may have problems with intimacy and be reluctant or unable to share feelings and thoughts with others. They may invest little or no emotional coin in social and romantic relationships. They will avoid intimacy by making up excuses such as tiredness and may not be concerned when a relationship breaks up. They may appear to move on straight away. They may also be unsupportive of a partner who is experiencing stressful times.

One observation we have made is that ambivalent types often seem attracted to avoidant types and vice versa! This seems to provide a guarantee of dissatisfaction in the relationship but also familiarity!

<u>Disorganised Attached Adults</u>
Much less has been written about the disorganised attachment style in adults. One characteristic seen in children (aged around six) with this style, is the behaviour of taking on a parental role with either of their parents or siblings. They become caregivers of the parent. It could be speculated that this might manifest in an adult relationship as controlling behaviour.

Bowlby believed there were four distinguishing characteristics of attachment:

- Proximity maintenance – the desire or drive to be near important care givers and attachment figures.
- Safe haven – the ability to return to the attachment figure when threatened or afraid for comfort and safety.
- Secure base – the attachment figure provides a safe base to venture out from to explore the surrounding environment.
- Separation distress – describes the type of anxiety that occurs in the absence of the attachment figure.

6. *Alfred Korzybski and 'the map is not the territory'.* To unpack the metaphor of 'the map is not the territory': if you look at an Ordnance survey map, you can recognise that the map represents the landscape. If you then went up in a helicopter above that same area you would not expect it to look the same as the map. You understand it is a representation of the landscape, a useful shorthand. See Korzybski, A (1958) *Science*

and Sanity: An Introduction to Non-Aristotelian Systems and General Semantics, Institute of General Semantics

7. **Unmet needs**. Our take on the nature of unmet needs was adapted (in the early 1990s) from Arthur Janov's Primal Therapy. See Janov, A. (1988) *The Primal Scream*, Abacus.

8. **Dr Phil McGraw and the 'soft place to fall'**. McGraw, P. (2000) *Relationship Rescue,* Simon & Schuster.

Chapter 3: Transforming Interactions

9. *John Gottman and the Four Horsemen of the Apocalypse.* (See Gottman, J.M. (2007) Why *Marriages Succeed or Fail,* Bloomsbury.) The four horsemen of the apocalypse and the counter horsemen are also relevant within a work environment. Dysfunctional relationships and teams follow the same model through avoidance, apprehension, antagonism and aversion. However, high performing teams seem to work the other way. Team members seek to discuss issues, welcoming difference and diversity as roads to innovation and progress. As they spiral upwards through the levels, they accept, appreciate and then admire differences in the team. When you hear someone from a high-performance team talking about a fellow team member it is usually respectful and complimentary.

10. *Paul Eckman and micro-expressions.* See Eckman, P. (2009) *Telling Lies: Clues to Deceit in the Marketplace, Politics, and Marriage,* WW Norton & Co.

11. *Fritz Perls quote.* Andreas, S. (1991) *Virginia Satir: The Patterns of Her Magic* Real People Press (p.53)

12. *John Gottman and the Seven Principles.* Gottman, J.M. (1999) *The Seven Principles for Making Marriage Work* Three Rivers Press (p.65)

Chapter 4: Becoming 'Balanced-Constructive'

13. ***NLP and Anchoring***. "In NLP, 'anchoring' refers to the process of associating an internal response with some environmental or mental trigger, so that the response may be quickly, and sometimes covertly, re-accessed." (Dilts, R.B. & Delozier, J.A. (2000) *The Encyclopedia of Systemic NLP & NLP New Coding Vol. 1,* NLP University Press, p29.) In a new relationship, we usually experience intense, fresh, new feelings associated with our new partner. It is likely that we will *also* be firing older anchors that are associated with love and relationships; these might range from excitement, joy and love to perhaps some less resourceful states like jealousy. 'Collapsing' an anchor occurs where one anchor is stronger than another. Both anchors are triggered at the same time and the stronger one wipes out the weaker one. If we naturally have strong positive anchors in our relationship we protect the quality of our connection with our significant other.

Chapter 5: The Readiness Factor

14. ***Two people pushing***. We were first introduced to this model by Graham Browne (Bellin Partnership/Universal Learning) on a series of personal development courses we attended in the early 1990s. Indeed, we met when we were on the 'support team' for one of the courses. Happy memories!

15. ***Men are from Mars***. Gray, J. (2002) *Men are from Mars and Women are from Venus,* Harper Collins.

16. ***Letting go of past flames***. This is a phrase/metaphor we use to help people to consider how they may be still 'holding a torch' for a previous love interest. In order to be with 100% present with their current partner, they may need to douse the old flames in order to make room for the *new* fire to ignite.

<u>Additional Notes</u>
In NLP (and beyond) there are a set of similar processes that can help to:

a) let go of past flames. Whether the previous relationship was loving or destructive, these processes can help gain a little distance and objectivity. They can also help with any guilt or self-deprecation someone might feel about themselves, as well as anger and resentment they may feel about the other person.

b) maintain a healthy relationship map with our current partner (and hence keep the interdependence between us). Not only do these processes help to give us 'unattached attachment' and freedom from 'neediness', they help to keep us in a clean and clear space with our partner.

These related processes are known as:
- <u>Releasing Co-dependency</u>: This process was developed by Steve and Connirae Andreas [Andreas, S. & C. (1989) *Heart of the Mind*, Real People Press]. Also known as Releasing Enmeshment [Dilts, R. & McDonald, R. (1997) *Tools of the Spirit*, Meta Publications].
- <u>Ho'oponopono</u>: According to Tad James, this process is from the ancient Hawaiian Huna [James, T. (1997) *Lost Teachings of Hawaiian Huna Vol. 1*, Advanced Neuro Dynamics].
- <u>Cutting the Ties That Bind</u>: A non-NLP process developed by therapist Phyllis Krystal [Krystal, P. (1982) *Cutting the Ties That Bind*, Turnstone].

The idea of these processes is to imagine letting go of the ties and attachments between yourself and another person. Remember that you are not rejecting the other person, but simply letting go of dependencies. In this way, it is easier to maintain interdependence.

Using Robert McDonald's approach as a template, the process begins with imagining another person and noticing a cord between yourself and that person. Consider severing the cord and notice any 'positive intentions' of (i.e. what you gain by) having the relationship. Imagine your own evolved self, standing by your side and gently release the cord from the other person and plug the 'open end' into your evolved self. Imagine the other person's evolved self, standing by their side and have them plug the other end of their cord into their own evolved self. Step into your evolved self and have the other person step into their evolved self. When this is done, imagine a time in the future where you might interact with that person and notice the positive changes.

17. *Social Panoramas*. See Derks, L. (2005) *Social Panoramas*, Crown House Publishing.

18. *Family of origin*. As a psychological term 'family of origin' appears to be connected with the work of Murray Bowen and his 'family systems theory'. We are particularly interested here in the concept of 'projection' where an adult carries an internal representation/'map' of their childhood family and uses that as a model for adult relationships, including 'seeking out' (unconsciously) the same relationship dynamics they had with siblings, parents and grandparents. We were introduced to the family of origin/projection link by Julie Hay. An interesting piece of research that has demonstrated a correlation between family of origin, attachment style and their effect on relationships in adulthood is: Dinero, Rachel E. et al. "Influence of Family of Origin and Adult Romantic Partners on Romantic Attachment Security." *Journal of family psychology: JFP : journal of the Division of Family Psychology of the American Psychological Association (Division 43)* 22.4 (2008): 622–632.

19. ***Transactional Analysis***. We would recommend the books of Julie Hay (e.g. *Working it out at Work*, 2009, Sherwood Publishing). Also, Ian S. & Vann J. (1987) *TA Today: A New Introduction to Transactional Analysis*. Lifespace Publishing, & Steiner, C. (1990) *Scripts People Live: Transactional Analysis of Life Scripts*. New York: Grove Press.

20. ***Neuro-linguistic Programming and changing limiting beliefs***. There is an NLP intervention called "change personal history" that allows us to reduce the power of old, negative automatic responses. We literally change how we think about life and the past. Old memories remain and anything we learnt from those experiences is preserved but the emotional impact is reduced. This frees us to make new choices and get new results. See Dilts, R.B. & Delozier, J.A. (2000) *The Encyclopedia of Systemic NLP & NLP New Coding Vol. 1*, NLP University Press, pp 157-159. Also, can be seen online: http://nlpuniversitypress.com/html/CaCom21.html

21. ***Finding a partner is luck***. See Wiseman, R. (2004) *The Luck Factor*, Century

22. ***Target rich environments***. See McGraw, P. (2006) *Love Smart*, Simon & Schuster

23. ***NLP presuppositions***. The NLP presuppositions have been pulled together from a variety of sources (e.g. Virginia Satir, Fritz Perls, Milton Erickson, Alfred Korzybski and Ross Ashby). We consider them to be 'empowering beliefs' and appear to us to be beliefs that are held (and acted upon) by folks who have the healthiest relationships.

Chapter 6: The Complementary Relationship

24. ***Robert Dilts and the 'neurological levels' model***. Dilts, R. (1990) *Changing Belief Systems with NLP*, Meta Publications.

25. ***Dr Phil McGraw and 'deal-breakers'***. McGraw, P. (2000) *Relationship Rescue*, Simon & Schuster.

Chapter 7: Communicating Relationships

26. ***NLP and metaprograms***. We would recommend reading Charvet, S.R. *(1997) Words That Change Minds*, Kendall/Hunt Publishing Company. For a more detailed guide, see: Hall, L.M. & Bodenhamer, B. (2005) *Figuring Out People*, NSP

Chapter 8: Relating through Difference

27. ***Equity theory and social exchange theory***. For the full article, see *Scientific American Mind*, Jan/Feb 2012 (or go to their website www.scientificamerican.com/mind)

28. ***Look into each other's eyes***: In couple's therapy, couples are often told to make eye contact with each other when complaining. This anchors bad feelings to the sight of each other, so every time they look at each other they will get the bad feelings. Virginia Satir used anchoring the other way around by having couples talk about when they first met "and when they start glowing, *then* she has them look at each other. She might say something like: 'And I want you to realise that this is the same person that you fell so deeply in love with ten years ago.' That connects an entirely different feeling." [Bandler, R. (1985) *Using Your Brain For A Change*, Real People Press, p12]

29. ***Synergy and self-actualisation***. See Hall, L.M. (2007) *Unleashed!* NSP (p.203)

30. ***NLP negotiation model***. See Dilts, R. (1980) *Neuro-Linguistic Programming: Volume I (The Study of the Structure of Subjective Experience)*, Meta Publications

Chapter 9: Revivifying Relationships

31. *NLP and love strategies*. Could also be called the 'language of love'. These are things we do for our partner to make them feel loved and the things we like them to do so we feel loved. In NLP, these strategies are sensory based (i.e. they are related to the five senses: visual, auditory, kinaesthetic, olfactory and gustatory).

32. *Little Prince/Princess syndrome*. The little prince/princess is a 'model of entitlement' (a concept we have been developing over the years but as yet not fully formed as a full model)...

    <u>Additional Notes</u>
A prince/ss tends to display a naivety about reality. S/he acts from the fantasy of how things *should/ought* to be and are less interested in how things really are. We call this the 'fantasy-reality' gap. S/he may avoid looking at how the world really works, how things really are and will avoid 'getting real' about their responsibilities (even looking at bank statements!) If things aren't how they 'should be', s/he may get angry with the world and sometimes take it personally. Ultimately, the prince/ss will struggle to enhance their true self esteem whilst they are stuck in a manipulative child-like world of wanting others to look after them.

    Typical phrases you will hear from a prince/ss:
- It's not fair
- I deserve it / I deserve better than this
- I should have a perfect world/everything I want
- I don't want that...
- I want a quick fix/magic wand...
- I can't/won't do that...
- *My* idea is better
- I wish that...

How can a prince/ss grow up and share responsibility in a relationship? If you recognise the pattern in yourself, the first step is about taking responsibility for your own experience, rather than needing someone/something to rescue you or expecting the world to be how it is not. Close the fantasy-reality gap by acknowledging that 'it is what it is' (and not 'how I think it should be'). There is no harm in helping to make the world a better place, but you need to take action (usually with others) to bring about the positive changes you would like to see in the world. Follow Gandhi's principle: be the change you wish to see I the world.

If you have goals (or want the world to be a particular way), consider this question: "how do you want to be different?" (i.e. what is your outcome?) Now, draw up a practical plan of action of how to get you there. If you don't like the idea of making compromises or sacrifices to get what you want in life, consider making 'investments' instead (e.g. in yourself, in your partner and in the relationship). Enjoy being responsible for the positive changes you experience... get creative!

33. ***Steve Andreas and conflict lies in comparison and seeking differences***. See Andreas, S. (2002) "*Transforming Your Self: Becoming who you want to be*" Real People Press (p38)

34. ***NLP and sub-modalities***. Sub-modalities are the qualities/finer details of our 'internal representations' (i.e. internal images, sounds, feelings). For example, if we imagine our partner and them speaking, what are the qualities of the imagery and the sound of their voice?

Imagery	Sound
Colour / black & white	Volume: loud / quiet
Brightness / dimness	Pitch: high / low
In/out of focus	Soft & gentle / harsh
Frame / no frame	Location of sound
Distance	Tempo: fast / slow

Size	Rhythm
Location	Melodious / grating
Movie / still	
2D (flat) / 3D	

The *way* we store internal representations tends to affect how we feel about the subject of our thoughts.

35. **Social Panoramas**. See Derks, L. (2005) *Social Panoramas*, Crown House Publishing.

Appendix

By Melody

Last year our dear friends, Tony and Justine got married. They were married at a registry office and wanted something more personal at their reception. They asked us to officiate an exchange of vows and they asked us to create a ceremony for them. We of course were delighted and touched that they asked us to do so.

In the months leading up to the wedding, Joe and I had a few discussions about what we might do but had not formulated anything specific. One morning I woke early with the whole thing fully formed in my head. I grabbed a note book and wrote it down.

The following pages are the template that I created based on our Relationship Dynamics model. I invited Tony and Justine to prepare their own vows using the following:

Vow Four: **There are many things I admire about you and here are three things I admire the most:**

I admire ......

I admire ......

I admire ......

My admiration of you is a reflection of the love I have for you, the honour that I hold you in and the promise of my continuing respect and loyalty.

What follows in the next few pages is the template we developed.

When two people join their lives together there is a transformation that occurs.

In the enlightened joining a new form emerges where each supports the other, allowing the growth of self where there is space to be truly yourself.

You can see and hear the other in all their magnificence and they can see and hear you. You are acknowledged for who you are, who you have been and there is a certainty that you will be acknowledged daily in your life together. And when you look into one another's eyes know that you are acknowledged, awareness exists.

There is an acceptance of your partners shadow, reflection, core and the mask they show the world. Your acceptance allows your partner to stand tall knowing they are safe with you. And you have the security to know that you are equally accepted.

Please face one another and hold hands, say together after me.

Vow One: **I see you, I hear you, you are acknowledged. I hear and I see that you acknowledge me.**

Vow Two: **I accept you in all your magnificence and all that makes you human. I hear and I see that you accept me.**

Vow Three: In acknowledging and accepting you my heart stays open, allowing me to appreciate how we are different and how we are the same.

As the transformation continues the enlightened couple can freely appreciate those aspects of each other that are the same and those that are different. Where there is sameness the connection is strengthened allowing shared values to be revealed. These shared values become the strong core of the relationship allowing you to stand united together.

The differences allow for individuality to be honoured and are a reminder that you are not two becoming one but two becoming independently whole. When two people are whole and complete they each bring strengths undiluted, creating a foundation on which to build a life that is fulfilling, enriching and nurturing. It allows you both the space and air to be yourself and the freedom to be together.

By appreciating one another in both difference and sameness you open the door to admiration.

Stand back for a moment and notice what it is you admire about this person you have chosen. Remind yourself every day, be confident in your admiration. Openly acknowledge, accept and appreciate what you admire. Telling your loved one what you admire will wrap their heart in warmth and tenderness so express your admiration often.

Just as importantly hear when you are admired in return. Allow an awareness and an acknowledgement of what you admire in your partner and what they admire in you. Appreciate your admiration as a flow in and out of energy between you that is a balance.

'A' please share with 'B' what you admire about him/her.

Vow Four: There are many things I admire about you and here are three things I admire the most:

I admire…

I admire…

I admire…

My admiration of you is a reflection of the love I have for you, the honour that I hold you in and the promise of my continuing respect and loyalty.

'B' please share with 'A' what you admire about him/her.

Vow Four: **There are many things I admire about you and here are three things I admire the most:**

I admire…

I admire…

I admire…

My admiration of you is a reflection of the love I have for you, the honour that I hold you in and the promise of my continuing respect and loyalty.

Could we have the rings please.

As you exchange rings as a traditional symbol of your union hold these vows dear.

Please say after me

Together we are transformed:

Pink ribbon

I am myself and you are aware of me.

Yellow ribbon

I am myself and you acknowledge me.

Orange ribbon

I am myself and you accept me.

Lilac ribbon

I am myself and you appreciate me.

Purple ribbon

I am myself and you admire me.

Together we are transformed into the best versions of ourselves.

And as you help one another untie the ribbons let that symbolise how you will help one another through life, and in the words of Kahlil Gibran

"Give your hearts, but not into each other's keeping.
For only the hand of Life can contain your hearts.
And stand together yet not too near together:
For the pillars of the temple stand apart,
And the oak tree and the cypress grow not in each other's shadow."

Ladies and gentleman, I present 'A' and 'B' as they begin this new phase of their life together.

About the Authors

Joe and Melody Cheal have been involved in the Personal &
Professional Development fields since 1993, gathering best practise
from all walks of life and business. They have personally trained and
coached over 20000 people, helping them revolutionise the way they
interact and work with others.

They met in 1992 and have been happily dancing together ever since!

Melody Cheal

Melody lives on the edge of Ashdown Forest, East Sussex with her husband, Joe and two dogs. She has a degree in Psychology, an MSc in Applied Positive Psychology, a diploma in Psychotherapy and is an NLP Master Practitioner and Certified NLP Master Trainer. She is a qualified Hypnotherapist and Hypnosis Trainer.

She is part of the external verification panel for the ANLP accreditation programme. Her Psychological Approaches to Coaching Diploma is accredited by the Association for Coaching.

She regularly speaks at national conferences and has presented her dissertation research, 'NLP and self-esteem', at an international research conference. Her work was published in an academic journal as a result. She is the author of *'Becoming Happy'* and the co-author of the popular books, *'The Little Book of Persuasion (Updated)'* and *'The Model Presenter'*.

Joe Cheal

Joe is the Lead Imaginarian and Trainer for Imaginarium Learning & Development. He has been involved in the field of management and organisational development since 1993. In focusing his training, coaching and consultancy experience within the business environment, he has worked with a broad range of organisational cultures, helping thousands of people revolutionise the way they work with others.

He holds an MSc in Organisational Development and Neuro Linguistic Technologies (his MSc dissertation was an exploration into 'social paradox'), a degree in Philosophy and Psychology and diplomas in Coaching and Psychotherapy.

Joe is an NLP Master Trainer who enjoys learning new things... by exploring diverse fields of science, philosophy and psychology and then integrating these 'learnings'. He is the author of *'Solving Impossible Problems'*, *'Who Stole My Pie?'* and the co-author of *'The Little Book of Persuasion (Updated)'* and *'The Model Presenter.'* He is also the creator and editor of the ANLP Journal: *Acuity*.

Training in Neuro-linguistic Programming (NLP)

NLP (Neuro-linguistic Programming) could be described as the psychology of excellence and the science of change. Through understanding more about how the mind/brain works (neuro) and how language affects us (linguistic), a practitioner is able to initiate and sustain change (programming) on a personal, interpersonal and organisational level.

NLP was designed originally to model excellence. By establishing exactly how someone achieves something, excellence can be modelled, taught to someone else and repeated again and again. From this starting point, over the last thirty years, an array of processes, concepts and techniques have been developed to enable you to:

- become more resourceful in managing attitudes, thoughts, emotions, behaviours and beliefs
- relate to others easily and effortlessly,
- understand how language and its use has a direct impact on your state, your brain and your success in communicating with others.

In addition to all this, as a GWiz NLP practitioner, you will learn techniques designed to help you develop your own skills and help others develop theirs. The principles will be introduced conversationally and with activities throughout the course allowing you to learn on many levels consciously and unconsciously.

As NLP Master Trainers we offer the complete three levels of certified NLP courses throughout the year:

- NLP 101
- NLP Diploma
- NLP Practitioner
- NLP Master Practitioner
- NLP Trainer's Training

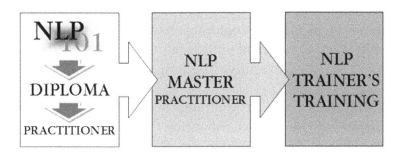

Our NLP courses are accredited through the ANLP.

We also offer Accredited Hypnotherapist training (through GHSC) from entry level through to Hypnosis Trainer.

As part of the ongoing support offered to all our students Melody provides supervision groups, mentoring and personal support to our graduates. This support is available to practitioners trained elsewhere.

If you are interested in personal and professional development and would like to more about NLP, have a look at our website: www.gwiznlp.com or contact us: info@gwiznlp.com.

Imaginarium Learning & Development is a consultancy that specialises in inspiring the natural potential of organisations, leadership, management and individuals through OD, L&D and Executive Coaching.

We work with clients from a broad range of sectors and aim to work in partnership with our clients, enhancing the profile of leadership, learning and development in our client's organisation.

Since 1993 we have experience of working with thousands of people from many organisations including:

Aeroflex, Amnesty International, ARA (Aircraft Research Association), Astra Zeneca & AstraTech, Autoglass, Avondale, Balfour Beatty, Bedford Borough Council, Central Bedfordshire, Beds Health, Beds Magistrates Courts Committee, Belron, Bio-Products Laboratories (BPL), Birdlife and Plantlife, British Gas, BT, Calderdale Council, Cambridge City Council, Cambridge University Press, Camelot, Cellnet, Central Bedfordshire, Church Conservation Trust, Cranfield University, Dixons Stores Group International, Emmaus Village Carlton, GSK, Herts Magistrates Courts Committee, Hertsmere Borough Council, Inland Revenue, J. Murphy & Sons, Langley Search & Selection, Lockheed Martin, London Borough of Camden, Luton Borough Council, Mercedes AMG High Performance Powertrains Ltd, Mylan, Newham Council, North Herts District Council, OAG, Olympic Blinds, RSPB, Sainsbury's, Santander, Serco, Shepherd Stubbs Recruitment, Staverton Park Conference Centre, The Assessment Network, Tesco, University of Hertfordshire, Welwyn Hatfield Borough Council, Welwyn Hatfield Community Housing Trust, Willmott Dixon, The Wine Society.

Imaginarium offers a range of consultancy services including:
- Learning & development / training courses
- Executive coaching and skills coaching
- Facilitation and team development
- Change management and organisational development
- Strategic engineering and paradox management
- Myers Briggs profiling and emotional intelligence testing

Our courses and topics include:

LEADERSHIP DEVELOPMENT
Change Management
Coaching Performance
Delegate!
Feedback for Effectiveness
Making Meetings Work
Management Development
Programmes
Managing People Successfully
Mentor Skills
Motivate!
Project Leadership
Team Building and Development

RESULTS AND RELATIONSHIPS
Assertiveness: Clarity and Focus
Building Partnerships
Communication
Conflict Resolution
Customer Care
Dealing with Aggression
Dealing with Difficult People
Handling Conflict in Meetings
Influence and Persuasion
Magic of Mediation
Negotiation Skills
Understanding Personalities

IN FRONT OF THE AUDIENCE
Advanced Presentation Skills
The Essential Presenter
Persuasive Presentations
Train the Trainer

PERSONAL IMPACT
Career & Profile Development
Coping with Change
Dealing With Pressure
Innovation: Getting Creative
Managing Your Performance
Staying Positively Happy
Stress Management
Time Management

EXECUTIVE DEVELOPMENT
Advanced Negotiation Skills
Becoming a Mentor
Beyond Selling
Making NLP Work
Managing Tensions
Organisational Development
Organisational Politics
Storytelling in Business
Strategic Change Management
Troubleshooting: Problem Resolution
Working with Transactional Analysis

HR SKILLS FOR MANAGERS
Appraisal
Capability & Disciplinary
Controlling Absence
Dealing with Poor Performance
Introduction to Counselling
Managing Difficult People
Recruitment Selection & Interviewing
Tackling Bullying & Harassment

Why work with Imaginarium?

Here are 4 things that make us special…

Experience

Imagine tapping into a wellspring of experience to help your people become more effective, more efficient and even more resourceful.

We have been involved in the learning & development environment for a quarter of a century! In the training and coaching environment, we have encountered and understood the majority of problems and challenges that human beings can face. We are able to draw from a wealth of practical resources, solutions, examples, models, hints, tips and ideas to help get people unstuck (and to help them 'unstick' themselves!) As individuals, we continue to learn and develop, keeping what we do fresh and engaging. We 'get' people!

Credibility

Imagine working with a company who regard your success and credibility as highly as their own.

We value not only our own credibility but also the credibility of the company we work with. We know that when we are training and coaching in your company, we represent "learning & development". We are passionate about advancing the reputation and culture of people development in organisations. We have worked with a vast range of organisational sectors and cultures giving us the ability to adapt from one company to another. We have also worked with some highly multicultural organisations, from people from all across the globe.

Humour & Enjoyment

Imagine your staff... keen to develop themselves
to become even better at what they do.

We love what we do! People who train with us enjoy themselves. We've been told that some people laugh and smile more in one day than they normally do in a week! We believe that enjoyment and light-heartedness are one of the most important keys to learning. Wherever we have embedded into an organisation's culture, people want to attend courses!

Return on Investment

Imagine working with people who care that
their service adds measurable value.

It is important to us that whatever we do, it adds value for your company. Sometimes this can be realised in terms of financial profits and savings. Sometimes return on investment is subtler in terms of staff motivation, efficiency and improved communication. Whether the returns are tangible or intangible we are keen to make sure that we are worth our weight in gold!

Psychological Approaches to Coaching Diploma

Accredited by the Association for Coaching

The programme is designed to allow learners time to reflect, consolidate and practice between modules. Each module is three days in length and includes supervised coaching practice with feedback.

For experienced coaches there is the opportunity to dip into the programme and attend individual modules. As this course is accredited by the Association for Coaches the modules can be used as CPD.

The modules are:
- Foundations in Coaching
- Transactional Analysis for Coaches
- Using the iNLP Coaching frame work
- Positive Psychology Coaching

Other Books from GWiz Publishing

Becoming Happy!
Lessons from Nature
By Melody Cheal

The search for happiness can often seem elusive and so this book provides hope for those wanting help in becoming happy.

Find out how to unlock the best version of you, recognising your own sense of worth and value. Melody shares experiences from her own journey of self-discovery plus tools and ideas she uses in her own practice.

The combination of pictures drawn from nature plus simple easy to apply exercises provides the reader with tools to begin transformation.

Are you ready to Be Brilliant?

Other Books from GWiz Publishing

WHO STOLE MY PIE?

By Joe Cheal

How to manage priorities, boundaries and expectations

Walter's lunch... and his time are being eaten into.

Fortunately, 'real-world' help is at hand to help him manage his time... and inadvertently, his pies!

Join Walter in learning how to manage priorities, boundaries and expectations...

Make your life easier and more fulfilling!

Who Stole My Pie is packed with powerfully simple models, tools, tips and techniques. If you want to gain greater control over your time then this book is for you!

Other Books from GWiz Publishing

the

MODEL
presenter

By Joe & Melody Cheal

The Model Presenter will show you how to:
- Develop the qualities of an exceptional presenter
- Create a memorable and logical structure
- Deliver presentations and training with confidence.
- Engage an audience easily and effortlessly
- Deal with a wide range of challenging situations

This 'how-to' guide is filled with steps to follow and helpful hints and tips modelled on
the best of the best.

You will discover a host of original material including:
* Closing the Gap between yourself and
the Mind of the Audience
* Preparing using the BROADCAST Model
* Delivering training sessions using
the IMPACT Formula
* Transforming nerves into confidence

Be remembered for the right reasons...
*As you become **the Model Presenter**!*

Other Books from GWiz Publishing

SOLVING IMP⊘SSIBLE PROBLEMS

By Joe Cheal

Say goodbye to organisational dilemmas, tensions, conflicts and stress with **Solving Impossible Problems***.*

The ability to manage tensions, paradox and uncertainty in business is becoming a much sought-after leadership skill.
'Paradox Management' is a new but increasingly essential field in the area of business management and will be highly influential in the ongoing sanity and success of all organisations and of the people who work for them.

Solving Impossible Problems will give you a greater understanding of organisational tensions and paradox. You will learn how to recognise these 'twisty turny' problems and then use practical tools to resolve them or use them for innovation.

This book is a unique guide to heightened wellbeing and enhanced thinking power through the revolutionary process of **Paradox Management***.*

Other Books from GWiz Publishing

THE LITTLE
BOOK OF
PERSUASION
UPDATED

By Joe & Melody Cheal

If you were more persuasive...

What would your life be like?
Where might you be and what might you have?
Where could you go and what could you achieve?

The Little Book of Persuasion is bursting
with practical idea for using anywhere.
Build relationships and get better results
at home, at work
and out in the big wide world!

For more information about
Joe & Melody Cheal,
Imaginarium Learning & Development,
GWiz NLP
and/or The GWiz Learning Partnership,
you can contact us at:

E: info@imaginariumdev.com
E: info@gwiznlp.com

Ph: 01892 309205

W: www.imaginariumdev.com
W: www.gwizNLP.com